Yola and the Yoles
Aidan Sullivan

First Printing, 2018
ISBN 978 1983196485

Contents

Preface

This is not a scholarly book, rather it is a short account of Yola and the Yoles, their dialect and traditions, but particularly their words and phrases.

It's a complex dialect, a word for apron, translates into three different Yola words, seaweed translates into several different Yola words, and there is another word for lake weed, limpet translates into two very different Yola words. *Unket* translates into 12 English words. Then there is the complexity of pronunciation, made all the more difficult in that the Yola speakers are all long dead, or so we were led to believe until 2018.

This is not a book to be read from cover to cover, rather, it is a loose reference book allowing readers to dip in and pick up Yola phrases, and general information on Yola lives of which very little is known, a unique tribe in the south-east of Ireland.

Introduction

Yola and the Yoles

A quaint dialect of old English was spoken only in south-east county Wexford in Ireland up until towards the end of the 19th century, and seemingly in a very small way into the 20th century. Called Yola, it was introduced to Ireland by soldiers, footmen, and army followers, who came with the Norman invaders in 1169. It lasted for centuries, not only as a language but as a small farmer way of life, with its own songs, dress, food, drink, dance, carvings, and customs, some of that language and tradition survives today. The language is thought to have evolved out of Middle English in the Chaucer and Shakespearean era, and was spoken in a slow drawl with unique pronunciation, "a" was pronounced slowly like as in *father*, or *faather,* a cake was a *caake*. To our ears today, Yola sounds like drawled Dutch, with pronunciation emphasising the second particle in a word, and in some cases the end of the word.

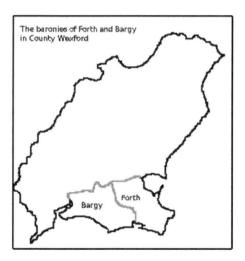

Figure 1 The location of Forth and Bargy in County Wexford (Wikipedia)

CULLENSTOWN CASTLE

DANESCASTLE, 1290

COOLHULL CASTLE (16th Cent.)

Figure 2 photos from A Parish and its People. The Normans built heavily fortified and moated castles such as the three above and centuries later built wide thatched mansions, or Big Houses, which were eventually slated.

Forth and Bargy

Yola means old, its speakers, Yoles. It was spoken only in the baronies of Forth and Bargy, in south-east county Wexford, an area of about 60 square miles, centred around Rosslare. Forth had a population, in the early 19th century, of around 24,000 and Bargy 13,000, a map (Figure 1) shows the baronies. These two adjoining baronies stretch from Taghmon, and the

Forth mountain down to Carnsore Point, the very southeastern tip of the country then westwards along the south coast of the county to Bannow Bay. That Bay and the river Pill form the western boundary of Bargy. The entire area was variously known as the *English baronies*, and the *Wexford Pale*. In 1850 the area was industrious and known as *Little Flanders* it boasted 24 windmills, far ahead of the usual Irish windmill count, an indication of the Yoles business drive. Bridgetown village, in Forth, had an unbroken history of milling stretching back for 600 years.

Bordering Yola into Forth and Bargy, insisted on by historians, may be too specific, the dialect surely did not end at the borders of those baronies and may well have spread beyond, such as into Shelmaleer, another barony that borders Forth to the northeast. The Normans, an invader tribe, later to become the Yoles had a strong initial commercial impact on the town of New Ross, far from Forth and Bargy. Indications are that some Yola was, at one stage spoken, or at least understood, in New Ross.

The Yoles did not use that name about themselves, neither did visitors to Forth and Bargy who referred to the people as Saxons, but it was the Irish who used the word, Yoles or Yols. Yoletown is a townland in Forth near Broadway village.

Over the centuries Yola was described as the *"old colonial English spoken in Ireland."*

Norman names in Wexford

The Yoles and their landlords brought Norman names to Wexford, including Devereux, Scurlock, Sinnott, Furlong, Godkin, Stacpole, Sutton, Fitzroy, Fitzgerald, Fitzhenry, Fitzstephen, Carew, St. John, Peppard, de Clarke, and Meyler.

Fitzgobert seems to be pre-Norman, from another invading soldier name, it may well be extinct in Wexford today, or again, could have evolved into Fitzgibbon.

Figure 3 Photo from the Centenary Record. This carefully posed photo is of wealthy Wexford shipping tycoon, Richard Devereux, a 19th century descendant of the original Devereux family that invaded with the Normans. Originally French, the family later settled in Wales, before they joined the Wexford invasion.

Some had prefixes which survive, thus we have the name, de Rope, or Roche, and la Roche, the la Roche name survives today, and de la Roche, or Roach, originally French. Hay is another Norman name, another version is de La Hay, a rare name in Ireland today.

Some Norman names are spelt in several different ways, *de Rope,* or *Rochfort* seems to be another version of Roche, as many as a dozen versions of a Wexford Norman name exist.

Other Norman names include. Esmonde, Hayden, Keating, Laffan, Marshall, Turner, Redmond. Rossiter, Neville, Lambert, Hore, Corish, and Colclough. Many of these names are common today in Forth and Bargy and in County

Wexford. The name Colfer is common in Bargy, less so in Forth. The Colfers congregated in Bargy, mainly in the south-west, in the Bannow area, there are few Colfers elsewhere in Ireland.

There are remote pockets in the barony of Forth, like Tachumshane, Lady's Island, and Carnsore Point, where this dialect was last spoken. It was also spoken in the Rosslare Fort, a small very isolated village at the mouth of Wexford harbour perhaps up into the 20th century. Historians kept repeating the various locations where Yola was, supposedly, last spoken in the 19th century.

Refreshingly, a credible report emerged in 2018, that some Yola was spoken up into the 1970 s in Forth. The surprise 1970's angle on the dialect, long after when it was supposed to have died, seems to have been missed by local historians. However, if it was discreetly spoken by only a few people or one family, it is understandable that it would not have come to the attention of historians.

Fortunately, Jacob Poole, (1774-1827) a Quaker farmer, from Growtown, near Taghmon, in Forth, collected 1,700 Yola words into his Glossary, or mini Dictionary, subsequently brilliantly edited and expanded, by T. Dolan and D. O Muirithe of University College Dublin in 1979 - without Poole, Yola would have been lost.

The foot soldiers and settlers who brought Yola to Wexford hailed from the West of England, and Wales, there were Flemish, Manx, and French, among them, some Irish seems to have been absorbed into Yola, quite a mix of language, pronunciation, and drawl, much of it spoken like the old English Wessex of Devon and Cornwall, and the old Saxon speech, as spoken along the Bristol Channel.

After Wexford surrendered to the Normans, the invaders got huge grants of land in County Wexford, top soldiers became landlords and their foot soldiers and settlers became their tenants with holdings typically from two to 20 acres plus. This was paying back time, the Normans had been invited in by Dermot MacMurrough, King of Leinster, to help him reconquer his land, and the Yoles got generous chunks of land as part of their deal.

The Yoles or Yols developed into a thrifty stay-at-home type of farmers, and hunter-gatherers, industrious, and sober, going to bed at 8 P.M. with 4.30 A.M. starts.

The Normans brought remarkable art to Wexford; this translated into magnificent stone carvings, such as a Norman Font, for a time in Bannow church, now in Carrig, it is pictured in this book, (Figure 8), an extraordinary font.

Cottages

The Yoles built small thatched cottages, these were unlocked as there was little or no crime among the Yoles, certainly no murders in the early centuries. The cabins were tidy, with outhouses for carts and animals. In earlier centuries the cabins would have been small circular one roomed, with animals brought in at night for safety from foxes and wolves. The one-roomed cottages had a high conical thatched roof, the earlier settlers slept in the rafters. Half of the house was for humans, the rest for animals, with a mud or sand floor it was limed, as were the walls made from special yellow mud. Most of the cabins were built without foundations.

Initially, these houses had only a door, or half door, there was no chimney, the smoke went out the door, and there were no windows.

Roofs were made of timber and straw or rushes. Recent research by University College Cork suggests a horrible depraved poverty-filled lifestyle for the early Norman settlers or Yoles, the smoke-filled dark damp mud cabins, killed children quite young and left many surviving children blind.

A hole in the roof later sufficed for a chimney, Yoles slept on straw woven into cloth pillows on the floor, or in the rafters. In subsequent builds centuries later, a spare wall shaded off the fireplace, and cooking was still carried out on the open fire, with utensils and pots hanging nearby from metal hooks. The fireplace and chimney, very much the centre of the house, had a spy hole, so those inside could see who was calling to their door.

Typical peasant's cottage.
After 1847.

Figure 4 Photo from, A Parish and Its People. This cottage scene, showing a near hovel is probably more realistic than the flowery descriptions of Yoles and their cottages in the 19ᵗʰ century painted by the likes of Bannow author, Mrs S.C. Hall.

In time some of the Yoles progressed to better than a one-roomed hovel, to two-roomed cottages, with a kitchen cum living room, with more sleeping space in the rafters. Some houses progressed to four rooms, but there was usually only a small window in each room, making the houses relatively dark, larger windows brought on higher rent demands from landlords. The windows in the early Yola houses did not open and were kept very clean. But a significant chunk of the Yoles never progressed beyond the one room basic mud cabin.

Furniture was basic and home built, cheap wood like deal was favoured for stools, chairs, and beds, couches doubled as *settle beds*, and though fast disappearing some are still found in very old houses.

Fireplaces tended to be wide, in some cottages two tiny benches were fitted into the fireplace, facing each other. These were two-seaters, and about only four feet wide, two in one fireplace opposite each other, at right angles to the fire. Some of these tiny benches are still about today, as first glance they look as if they are minute church pews, instead, they fit neatly into the fireplace. There was a slot in the chimney used for seasoning wood which was then used to make spokes, furniture, and boats. There was a drain under the house from the back to the front, it was connected with the fireplace, and provided a draft no matter what the direction of the wind.

What we now call an Irish dresser, took pride of place in the kitchen. Hens were often kept in two bottom drawers, with the hens on top, while the eggs fell down into lower drawers Dressers were made of wood and were home built, and usually painted white, others in a mix of colours.

The prosperous built timber trunks used for storage, and a luxury in coastal areas were ships trunks, occasionally recovered from shipwrecks, or found washed up on beaches.

Figure 5 photos are used with permission from A Parish and Its People. Some of these remarkable thatched cottages survive today.

Landlords lived in thick walled fortified castles, often 60-foot-tall, some had moats, some survive today, and are occupied after hundreds of years. Outside of New Ross, two families now live in a divided Norman castle, there are others living in these very old structures today.

Landlords built comfortable wide mansions starting in the 1400's and most, but not all of the Norman castles were abandoned. Photos of some of the mansions, or Big Houses, in Bargy, are displayed in this book, including Harristown House, a thatched mansion built in 1715 (Figure 19).

The Yoles grew flowers to the front of their cabins and were on good terms with their landlords, tenants were often found at their landlord's table. Yoles were Catholics, short, broad-shouldered with Roman noses and dark eyes, and oval faces, the women had good skin and were better looking than the Irish.

The Yoles were moderate drinkers of alcohol, they consumed far less than the neighbouring Irish, who drank to excess.

The Yoles built their churches near their landlord's castle, some castles enclosed a church, there was a heavy concentration of Catholic churches in Forth and Bargy. Initially, these churches were small mud cabins, Figure 24 captures the Catholic mud cabin church, but as castles were abandoned churches were built from the castle stones. There is a high concentration of holy wells in Forth and Bargy, but holy wells were not originated by the Yoles.

Yola Food

All of the diet was home produced augmented by hunting, fishing, and gathering. The main food was stirabout, or porridge and milk, or buttermilk, which was drunk with every meal. The Yoles even milked their sheep and gave goats milk to sick children. Beans and potatoes made up the rest of the diet. The poor could not regularly afford wheaten bread, a luxury food eaten occasionally. The Yoles had special foods, including, *Buskes*, a spiced cornbread. Cabbage, turnips, and fish, were part of the diet. Those living by the coast fished in the sea, some part-time, and harvested shellfish from rocks and pools, others fished in rivers, lakes, and ponds. With a variety of food sources, the Yoles were relatively insulated from the ravages of the Famine in the 1840's, when the potato crop badly failed their neighbouring Irish.

Pork, beef, wild birds, rabbits, and hares, were part of their diet. For some reason the Yoles were slow to get into rearing and slaughtering cattle, instead, pigs predominated. These were larger and wilder than the pigs bred today, just how modern pigs got to be smaller is unexplained. Meat, fish, poultry, and game were smoked over the Yola fire and stored in the chimney.

Smoked food was preserved for quite some time, as long as a year.

The Normans introduced rabbits to Ireland.

Pigs were the main animal on small farms. Weeds were a feed for pigs, together with waste food from houses. Poor Yoles, with little acreage, steered their pigs onto roadways and beaches to graze. The pig was tethered by a short rope attached to a back leg, 19th century paintings illustrate this tether.

Pigs were slaughtered by cutting their throats with a knife, a noisy and painful, but brief ritual, the blood was salvaged to make pudding.

In time the Yoles took to brewing tea. Coffee was to come along later, Forth and Bargy were slow to embrace coffee, another new beverage, after hundreds of years on milk, buttermilk, and home-brewed ale, beer, and poitin, a raw concentrated version of Irish whiskey.

The Yoles picked wild fruits, blackberries, loganberries, wild raspberries, elder berries, fraughan berries, haws, sloes, mushrooms, chestnuts, wild juniper, and edible flowers. Heather, hops, and flowers, including the flowers of gorse, were used to brew alcohol. Hops grew wild in Forth and Bargy, some still grow wild there today, and are currently used in brewing, as they were over the centuries.

The Yola women were the brewers, and they introduced the children to ale and beer.

Crops

Before the Normans came the Irish were mainly pasture farmers allowing their animals to graze, the Yoles quickly changed all that and grew crops, they went far further and introduced crop rotation, which was very advanced at that time. It helped that Forth and Bargy had a mild climate, boosted by being bordered by the sea.

Potatoes grown on the Carne peninsula, in Forth, were ready for harvesting far ahead of the rest of county Wexford, and much of the rest of Ireland, due to its proximity to the sea, and a lake, on three sides.

Barley was sown during the last week in March and the first week of April; the seed was put into a tall narrow wicker basket, made from straw and briar. That basket had an arm or handle in the middle, the sower held the basket near the inside of his elbow and threw the seed far in front of him.

The Yoles kept their own seeds in a sheaf until March they were then taken out and threshed ahead of planting.

Some hemp and flax was grown, seemingly in small volumes

Tobacco growing in Forth

Tobacco was a lucrative crop introduced by the Yoles after 1815 it rapidly became a boom crop, fetching £100 to £150 an acre, priced far above other crops, and spawning a tobacco processing factory in Wexford. Just how the Yoles hit on tobacco, sourced the initial plants, and got the know how to grow tobacco, is unclear, but thousands of acres of tobacco seem to have been grown, raising the standard of living of the Yoles, allowing them to buy small luxuries. However, in 1831, England moved to outlaw tobacco growing in Ireland, with an Act of Parliament, leading to its rapid demise.

This was the Government of the Whig Prime Minister, Charles Grey, now best remembered, for giving his name to Grey's tea.

Figure 6 British Prime Minister, Grey, above, wrecked the tobacco growing industry in Forth in 1831, for no good reason.

Just why he and his government felt threatened by relatively small tobacco growing in the south-east of Ireland is unclear, but the role of Edward Smith Stanley, Chief Secretary for Ireland, must have been pivotal, he was a member of Greys Cabinet. How both felt threatened by, in Empire terms, the relatively small growing of growing of tobacco in Wexford is not clear.

In the 20th century, an effort was made to restart tobacco growing in Forth. Ireland was then a free country, so the prohibition imposed by England did not apply. The new tobacco plants grew without a hitch, but seemingly the blend was not to the tobacco markets liking, and tobacco growing was again sadly abandoned. Some signs of 20[t] century tobacco growing survive, such as an unusual barn type structure with distinctive black painted heavy timber walls, just outside Killinick in the direction of the rail station.

History today quite rightly smiles on Grey for his anti-slavery legislation and Smith Stanley for paving the way for the establishment of national schools in Ireland, that same history does not explain why they wrecked the Yoles promising tobacco industry.

It may well have been yet another effort to keep the Irish, or more specifically, the Yoles, down.

The Wexford historian, Dr George Hadden, proposed the growing of soya beans in the 20th century, it is not clear whether soya growing was ever attempted.

Reaping crops

Before a hook was taken to the barley crop the wind direction was first ascertained, then the harvester put the wind to his back. The wind blew the corn away, and the harvester could go after the butt. Three cuts yielded a fistful, which were tied into sheaves, and left in the sun for a week.

Women were employed as barley cutters, there are reports that they were paid as much as men, a surprise as the Yoles were a male dominant society. The last sheaf to be cut was known as a *bunyuck* in the Bannow area of Bargy.

When the harvest was complete the farmer threw what was called *head,* a party where drink flowed freely, and dancing continued throughout the night, drinking and dancing all night was a strong Yola tradition.

Winnowing was carried out by men and women. It involved holding a sieve-like device on the head, the sieve was filled with corn, the wind blew away the chaff, and the corn fell to the ground. Taller people were said to get better results from the winnowing process.

Bean growing

The growing of beans in Wexford was introduced by the Yoles so much so they were known as "Beaney boys". To grow them, a field was first ploughed with a wooden plough or dug with spades. It next was harrowed using a wide piece of wood into which nails were driven, the plough and harrow was drawn by four horses. Ridges were dug into the newly harrowed field, and manure or seaweed put into the ridges, then beans were thrown in on top of the manure, and the beans were covered in clay. The growth of the beanstalks indicated the beans were ripening, the stalks were cut into bunches, and brought into a haggard for threshing, a task for two men. The stalks were burned in the fire.

Some of the bean crop was sold, the balance was kept as household food, and served with potato and salt. The Yoles were fortunate to have beans when the potato crop failed in the 1840's, their Irish neighbours did not grow beans and starved when the potato crop, their sole food, failed.

The Yoles also grew peas.

They cultivated every scrap of their land, there were no fields under weeds or water, as is often the case today.

Hiring time and Hiring Fairs

The Yola farms were small and only supported one family, adult males who did not inherit the lease had to find work. They stood outside church gates after Sunday Mass hook in hand, offering their labour to cut and save crops .The hired man moved from farm to farm until the harvest was completed, there could be 20-30 men working in a field in an era prior to mechanisation, using scyths and hooks.

Quite different to Church gate hiring, there also *hiring fairs* where dozens of men were examined by employers. They were usually hired from May Day to May Day of the following year and lived with the farmer for that year at the end of which they were paid a lump sum, enough for some to take a lease on a farm of their own, or emigrate, England being the preferred destination for centuries.

The fate of hired men on farms varied, some found the farmer-employer to be kind, others cruel.

Hiring fairs died out in Forth and Bargy, but continued later in places like County Limerick up until the 1950's.

A change in Yola farming in the 17th century

Yola farming, and hunter-gathering, remained quite remarkably unchanged over the centuries, however, in the second half of the 17th century, the benefits of applying lime to the land were recognised giving birth to lime kilns.

Groups of farmers, probably with the blessing of their landlord, combined to build a kiln, using stones from derelict castles and churches. Some individual farmers built a kiln on their land, the kilns were sturdy structures capable of withstanding considerable heat.

Crushed limestone rocks were put into the kiln and a fire lit at its base, the considerable fire was kept going, for several days, until the rocks melted to yield lime, which was then mixed with seaweed and manure, then spread on the land. Many of these old rock chimneys survive today, such as the kiln near the bridge over the Slaney at Killurin, seemingly a co-op type kiln built on commonage, as were many of the kilns in Forth and Bargy.

Around this time the industrial revolution was underway in Britain, a smaller one was to follow in Ireland.

Getting the grain to market

After threshing the grain had to be carted to markets such as Wexford. Depending on the distance from the town a farmer set off at midnight or later walking beside his horse. Barley was carried in 20 stone sacks, four or five sacks per cart. There was generally a stop a few miles outside the town, Judy Doyles of Traceystown was a favoured pub stop with those coming a long distance from the west of Bargy, that journey would have been started at late night or dawn.

At Judy Doyles, they were met by porters employed by grain buyers from Wexford who jumped up on the cart and took a fistful of grain as a sample for their employer. Farmers put their better grain to the top of the sack to hoodwink buyers.

The carts then made for Wexford, at Bishopswater on the western edge of the town where they were met with buyers, bidding started quite soon.

Grain crops had brought prosperity to Forth, Bargy, and Wexford, mills sprung up. A Mill Road sprung up on the Bishopswater river, and another mill in Peter Street, the historian Billy Colfer tells us in his book, Wexford. By 1840 there was a brewery at the corner of Peter Street, and Main Street, and other breweries at Maudlintown and Spawell Road. There was a considerable cluster of 14 windmills on the hill now known as Belvedere Road, they were shown in a map of the town dated 1770. That area became known as Windmill Hills, and a rug making business located in the area used the postal address, Windmill Hills, up into the 1970's.

There is little trace of these mills today, in the 1970's a ruin of one of these mills existed in nearby Coolcots, in a lane now gated off, it is unclear whether some of it remains today, or whether it is overgrown or demolished. There is no trace of another mill located near the Booker Christian Brothers school in the town. The ruins of a windmill are visible today near the Lobster Pot pub in Carne, and there are many other such ruins in south-east Wexford, some can be seen off the New Line road, which runs westwards from Wexford, through Forth, and then into Bargy to Wellington Bridge.

Remains of 19th century Windmill, Kiltra.

Remnant of 17th century Windmill or Look-out Post, Cullenstown.

Figure 7 Photos from a Parish and its People. Windmilling was a large industry in Forth and Bargy, such was the high number of windmills that the two areas were known as Little Flanders.

Water mills date back to the 13th century, streams were harnessed to grind crops, there are fine examples of water mills at Castlebridge and nearby Garrylough on the Wexford-Gorey road, neither is in use, they are outside of Forth, but not that far outside, about three to five miles northeast of Wexford on the east side of the Slaney river.

There were mills on various rivers of which we have little or no trace of today. There is a river that flows through Killinick in Forth, that river, travels near the derelict Killinick railway station, and hosted five mills, each hived off a water supply from the river, and stored it in a pond, drawing down water as needed. Those ponds and mills, located around Killinick, have reverted to nature today.

The pond powered mill was a clever development for its time. Forth is relatively flat, gradually, very gently sloping down from the Forth mountain to the south, and the sea, it lacks roaring streams, in contrast to neighbouring county Wicklow and Carlow, where streams tear down at speed from mountains. So, the pond powered mill, was a local clever Yola invention, to fit the needs of the flat area.

A tidal mill seems to have been envisaged near Bannow, in recent years a large timber wheel was recovered from mud, near Tintern, leading to speculation it was used to harness tidal power. It is unclear whether this tidal mill ever operated, it may have been built by, or at the behest of Tintern monks, known for progressive ideas.

Figure 8 The first two photos are from A Parish and its People, the third is from a History of Lady's Island

The Norman Font above left gives us an idea of the Yola stone carving skills, Right top, is an empty stone coffin indicating wealth, or perhaps a military figure. Lower right is Lady's Island lake, the Yoles extracted weed from this lake as fertiliser, they were also prominent in its 15th of August pilgrimage.

Yola farms sold animal skins to tanneries in Wexford, there were six tanneries located in John Street, it is unclear why tanning in Wexford died out. Small animal skins were cured at home and used to line boots, fox skins were used to make coats. Fox heads with the skin attached were worn by women above the breast, the fashion of wearing of fox skin, mainly by older women, continued up into the 1960's. Some fox heads were incorporated into women's hats, but this died out in the mid-1960's but is undergoing a revival today among fashion-conscious young women in Europe. Some of it Punk fashion, some of it very far from Punk. Fox skins and heads are once again valued, some beautifully dyed fox skins are used as collars attached to expensive dresses, in fashion with a minority, in Europe, but not in Ireland.

Malt stores

Flourishing mills in and near Wexford created a new industry, malting and malt stores, most of them four storey brownstone buildings. Processed grain was stored in these buildings and then sent by ship to distillers and brewers in Dublin and England.

There was a peak of a considerable 38 malt houses in Wexford in 1831, after that date amalgamations seemingly reduced that number.

Malting thrived in Wexford for centuries and continued up into the 1970's. Malt stores were then mainly converted into apartments, old brownstone buildings, usually four stories, in Peter Street, Paul Quay, Upper King Street, and the Faythe.

Yoles Dress and Enteete

The swarthy men wore round hats with a narrow brim, a waistcoat, short trousers, and socks up to the knee. Women wore caps or scarves on the back of their heads, others rolled cloth around their heads turban style. They wore frocks tied at the waist with ribbons, petticoats, and a cloak, usually blue, and a bonnet for outside. They wore *scolyoons* or aprons, also called *prankeens*, and other names, such as *praiskeens.* Some aprons were chosen for selected tasks on the farm; all these were homemade from jute.

A painting reproduced in Figure 25 gives us some idea of how the Yoles dressed in the mid-1640's. Though the painting is Flemish, it is more than likely the Yoles dressed the way of the Flems.

Some of the adult Yoles wore home built clogs carved from lumps of wood.

In 1938, Dick Maddock, of Ballygow in Bargy, then aged 87, described his own home when he was growing up.

> *I remember a spinning wheel in the house where I was reared, but I never remember seeing it working. The quilting frame was always in use as long as my mother lived, she always made all our clothes. She used to make hats from straw or rushes. The women made some of the finest patchwork quilts in those days.*

Yola men were dominant, the women served the men first; if the husband was not present the eldest son was served first, or else a manservant. The poorer houses ate meat twice a week, and it was traditional to all Yola houses to take a Siesta, or *Enteete* in the afternoon. That Siesta tradition was so well observed that practically no one was on the roads or could be seen in the Yola area during slumber time, it survived into the 20th century. That Siesta was also called a *Nonteet*, or noon rest. Some authors got carried away in their description of the Yola Siesta and argued that the farm animals and poultry slept during that time, along with their owners, those who wrote about the animals having a Siesta may have been drinking the local poitin, or Irish moonshine.

Some of the Yoles ate a *Risheen*, a small snack between dinner and supper. Women workers did the same farm work as men, except ploughing, the farms grew a spectrum of crops including beans, grain, potatoes, and flax, and were less exposed when the Potato Famine came in the 1840's. Beans were part of their diet, they hunted and gathered, whereas most of Irish depended entirely on potatoes, the Irish were left to starve when the potato crop failed in the 1840's.

The Yoles did not stray far from home instead they lived quietly, mostly within their parish. They were clean, well clad, properly behaved, and lived in neat cabins, with flowers planted to the front.

Reports by visitors confirm Yola women were paid the same wages as men for their farm work, a contrast to their neighbouring Irish women, who are still today fighting for gender pay equality. Writers focused on Irish feminism do not mention the Yola women getting equal pay, probably because so little is known about the Yoles. The origin of the gender pay equality among the Yoles is unknown, but it seems to be unique in Ireland, if not Europe.

Thrifty, the Yoles harvested sea and lake weed called *wore* or *landruch, or landruck,* (and other Yola names) as a fertiliser, generally in the Spring, April, and May. Some landlords had control over lakes or ponds and would only allow the Yoles to cut weeds in daylight. There are old reports of tenants harvesting shore and lake weed at night. That was probably an exceptional bullying landlord, who for his own reasons prohibited weed harvesting during daylight, but generally, landlord-tenant relations were good, though there would have been a huge economic and educational gap between the two.

Figure 9 from the National Gallery of Ireland. The Yoles harvested weed from the sea, lakes, and ponds, using it as fertiliser. This painting by Joseph Malachy Kavanagh records this, the Yoles confusingly, used several words to describe sea and lake weed.

Seaweed was used as a fertiliser, it was also used in thatching, and a weed special to Wexford Harbour was exported to England, where it was used in upholstery.

Fairs

The Yoles sold their crops and animals in towns like Wexford through fairs in the Faythe, Bannow, and Taghmon. Apart from the trade in animals and birds, a spectrum of food and homespun clothes, and blankets were sold at fairs, together with seeds, farm gear, and equine items like *pilleens* or women's saddles. The fair was an opportunity for a household to sell something, to make money, it was also a regular social occasion, nearby pubs opened at 7 a.m.

Figure 10 from a painting by Gladys Maccabe, from Whyte's Dublin art auctioneers catalogue. Fairs were held monthly and allowed people to sell their produce along with animals.

Horses, donkey and carts, and pony and traps provided transport, the Yoles bred sturdy Forth mountain ponies, in demand from all over Ireland. That breed, with exceptional spirit and strength, seems to be dead today. It is not clear why this breed died out, all the more so when there was strong demand. It may be that name, Forth mountain was ditched, as the Yola dialect and way of life fell apart, but the ponies survived, this is unclear.

The Yoles also bred horses on the limestone land in Forth and Bargy, their landlords hunted on horseback, while their tenants were more likely to have hunted foxes with beagle dogs on foot.

Travelling by horseback was common, and a trip to Dublin was more often undertaken by sea, it was cheaper, safer, and faster, and centuries ago dodged highway robbers and murderers.

Small ships, as many as 30, operated out of one tiny port like Bannow, in Bargy, running up to Dublin, Wexford was also a bustling port, with Dublin, Welsh, and English destinations. One of the very few to record commuting from Bargy to Dublin by sea was the novelist, Mrs S.C. Hall, who grew up and lived in Bannow until she was 14, as Ann Fielding. She had been born in Dublin, after her father died she moved to relatives in Bannow she records such a trip by sea with her mother to Dublin in the 19th century.

For centuries, Yola was the mother tongue of the poorer classes in Forth and Bargy, yet there was no friction between the Yoles and the Irish. Rather the Yoles, or Yols, kept to themselves and did not integrate with the Irish. Of the original invaders, most knew each other, many were related.

However, most of the very first wave of Yoles, the footmen, back in 1169, were single men, and some must have married Irish girls, such unions solidified Catholicism into Yola culture. The invaders brought with them their own chaplains who became the first priests among the Yoles.

Some elderly Yola men carried a walking stick, often a blackthorn, very few of them used a stick to conceal a sword or single barrel shotgun because they were peaceful. In very recent years an elderly man in Wexford almost always used a thick walking stick, but it was not generally known that this stick, called a *bat*, hid a shotgun. That tale ended tragically.

Repeated suggestions by historians that the Yoles were a subservient underclass, tend to grate as if somehow, we should be embarrassed about them. Sure, they began in Wexford as invader foot soldiers, with little to lose, the higher military ranks were given Irish land for their services, but there is nothing to suggest that the Yoles were stupid, rather the opposite, they were clever people, and contributed extensively to the prosperity of their adopted, Forth and Bargy, as they do today.

There were few Protestants among the Yoles, less than one in 100, and about the same number of Irish speakers. Some reports suggest there was no Irish whatever spoken in the two baronies, but Irish was unlikely to have been exterminated overnight. Instead, the Yoles probably took on scrub, bushy, land, cleared it, and some of the initial single footmen married into the Irish, but such unions were probably rare, instead the soldiers married into the followers who came with the invaders.

It may have been that the Yoles felt more comfortable in the midst of other ex-soldiers, followers, and their way of life. Poverty and the grinding lifestyle of small farming over the centuries kept them down, the Yoles were, and are, patronisingly regarded as an underclass by the Irish.

Some historic reports suggest the Yoles were already an underclass in the West of England, Wessex area, and just continued that role in the south-east of Ireland. It is suggested they had little to lose by joining the invasion of Ireland. Historians keep repeating this underclass line, yet there is some unexplained sensitivity today in even mentioning the Yoles, delicately fingered by Shane Dunphy, a Wexford historian, in a radio documentary, for RTE, the State broadcaster.

The Yoles brought with them not only farming skills, but a spectrum of basic trades, from hunting, fishing, house building, to brewing, and distilling. Also, they brought their traditions, folklore, music, carving skills, and dress.

What the Yoles made at home

They made their own ale and beer, served from *Jocks* or buckets made from cowhide, black sheep were favoured, they processed flax into linen, usually on their own farm, but there were also flax processors, operating what was called a *green room*. They also made *poitin*, or illegal whiskey, that tradition continues in a discreet way today. Households created for their own needs, ink, dyes, candles, soap, sacks, ropes and starch, bread, butter cheese, cakes, and preservatives, they spun wool, and weaved, made all their own clothes, blankets, shoes, shoelaces, killed cured and smoked their own meat and poultry, and grew their own vegetables.

Figure 11 From the Journal of the Wexford Historical Society, M. Conboy, 1968, a dash churn, used for butter making on smaller farms.

Not all of the Yoles were subservient to landlords, there was land rent free available on the Forth mountain, a 700-foot hill that gazed down onto south County Wexford, at its peak are three rough rocks, giving the Forth Mountain another name, Three Rock Mountain. But it needed to be cleared, and after that, it was poor land. It attracted horse breeders, who gave their name to the aforementioned Forth Mountain pony. The Forth mountain towered over otherwise flat land, it became a weather beacon for those living below. If there was dirty cloud and rain on Forth, it was likely coming their way soon. It was the only mountain that the Yoles of Forth could view.

Few of those living under the shadow of the Forth mountain bothered to walk up it, the Yoles were very much stay-at-home folk, keeping largely within the parish. But a Yola woman did make the trek to the top and gazed north to see Taghmon and the flat land leading on the river Slaney to the east. She was so taken aback by this view that she vowed never to climb the Forth Mountain again.

Contemporaneous Records of the Yoles

A visitor to Forth and Bargy in 1682

Over the centuries several visitors have left us a record of how the Yoles lived, among them **Solomon Richards,** a Cromwellian planter who left us this account.

It was an observance of the inhabitants of Forth and Bargy before the last rebellion of 1641, that they kept their language, lands, and loyalty, having seldom nor never married but among themselves, having never rebelled until 1641. They were mainly freeholders but their freeholds were very small, and never being forfeited remained as they were first set out and divided by Fitzstephens soldiers in 1170. The soil is naturally coarse and barren, yet, by the industry of the people, together with the congruity to the sea, which they bring ouse, or seaweed, with which they manure their cultivated lands, it is made the garden of the country.

They breed few or no cattle.

The men are of low stature yet well set, thick and strong, crafty and deceitful enough, few of them scholars but those that do excel. At high noon, not only men and women, but children also servants cease work and labour and go to rest for an hour or two.

At two they rise and continue their several works until six when they return to their houses, make merry with their families over a super provided for them by their industrious wives, and retire about eight. They train up their children early to industry, disobedience to parents is counted as most atrocious and never-to be-forgotten crime. They commonly dispose of their offspring very young the boys marry at 18 to 20, the girls 14 to 18.

He wrote the above in 1682 and also left us an account of Wexford in that year. He details the former booming herring fishing industry in the town and its decline.

An account of life in Forth and Bargy in 1684

A man called **Sinnott** left us the following account, he may well have been a local man. His first name is not known, he may have been a Catholic priest.

> *They take moderate refection at morn, noon, and night. They are very vigilant so that the sun cannot surprise them in bed and, recommending themselves to God, they set to work. In summer they stop work around 11 A.M. and soon after, dine, reposing until about two o' clock. They celebrate with singular pious devotion the yearly feasts or patron days in honour of God and his saints and invite their neighbours and friends to their houses where they entertain with the best accommodate the country can afford. They are very precise and exact in observing all the enjoined feasts never eating meat on Fridays or Saturdays, few using eggs, butter or milk on Fridays, and abstaining always from meat on Wednesdays. This went on until 1670, when they were dispensed from rigorous fasts. They make some wonderful beer and wholesome ale, they also distil aquae vitae, not inferior to any in Ireland. They are of good complexion firm constitutions and great maturity of years, they are honest and candid with strangers and no robberies or felonies are committed among them, and there are no vagrant beggars.*

He leaves us the following description of Yola landlord houses

> *The mansion houses of the gentry were fortified with castles some nearly sixty feet high, having walls at least five foot thick, of quadrangle form of which very few*

have yet become ruinous. Their houses were built with stone walls, slated, having spacious halls, in the centre of which were fire hearths according to the English mode, all houses at present having chimneys.

Plebian (or poorer) people have their habitations completely built of mud, so firm and high they frequently raise lofts thereon, neat, well accommodated with all necessary implements.

Another account of life in Bargy in 1684

Robert Leigh was a landlord, living in Rosegarland, Bargy, he wrote,

They retain among the common people the old or Saxon language and customs, and keep to their old way of worship or religion.

They keep their land well fenced in small enclosures and stick to their old habitations or places of birth though never so much imposed on by their new landlords (after 1654) so they are now become tenants to those who had the land confirmed to them by the Act of Settlement (1652 and 1662)

Remarkably, the Leighs continue to live in Rosegarland today, few landlords in Forth and Bargy have lasted as long as this family.

Amyas Griffiths visits Wexford in 1764. He wrote:

Before Cromwell's time the town was well enclosed, part of the walls are yet standing, with four gates, one at each quarter of the town. The Main Street from the Westgate to the Barrack Gate about three-quarters of a mile in length. Outside of the Westgate is a fine spa reckoned by skilful physicians to be an infallible cure for many disorders, among them scurvy, gout, and decay. It creates an appetite and dispels melancholy. Beyond the South Gate stands the barracks, a large, low building, forming a little square. I have heard it can contain four companies completely. From this barracks runs a very broad street upwards of a mile in length named the Fierth, commonly style the Faith. The cabins which compose this suburb or outlet are very snug and commodious, and the dwellers are a set of the most industrious people on the earth. Their employments are mostly weaving nets or spinning hemp.

In the midst of heart of the main street is the Bullring, where the courthouse with an excellent clock stands. About 50 yards from the courthouse, southwards, is the new church, which when finished in miniature will come nigh in beautiful structure, workmanship, materials, to any in Dublin. Between the church and the barracks, a little above Jews Bridge, lies the gaol. It is but ordinary but built exceedingly strong with a courtyard. In John Street, north west of the town, is the chapel; it is one of the prettiest I have ever seen, with a friary and garden belonging to it. The chapel yard is esteemed the best walk about the town. We have a prodigious number of other streets, lanes, and quays, the Flesh Market, Cornmarket, Back Street, Shambles, Kaisers Lane, Ferryboat Quay, Meadows Quay, Bennets Quay, Common Quay, Gibsons Lane, the Custom House Quay, which is the chief or principal of all the other quays, half of which I have not mentioned. The Custom House Quay is small, but vastly pretty with seats all round, a good warm watch house, and an excellent custom house, with convenient stores.

I procured the number of houses in the town at 1300 and in the confines of the walls 650 slated houses. For ale and oysters Wexford is noted as having the best on earth. The chief exports are corn, herrings, beef, beer, hides, tallow, butter, they trade to all parts of the globe, but in particular to Liverpool, Barbados, Dublin, Norway, and Bordeaux. Wexford imports, brandy, rums, sugars, wines, dyestuffs, porter, fruit of all foreign kinds, salt, timber, and hops.

Wexford is celebrated for its fine women, beer, and oysters.

A visitor to Bargy in 1776

Arthur Young, described as an agriculturalist, visited Bargy, this is his description,

Cattle are little attended. Each family has only a cow or two with a few sheep, but they keep a great many pigs.

He says they brought the pigs to graze on beaches. He also records that products made by Yola wives by spinning and weaving were sold at fairs, included were flannels, coarse linen, and linsey. The Yola households also produced what known as linsey woolsey, seemingly a mix of linen and wool. The Yoles were keen to harvest seaweed, some put it quickly into the soil, other farmers let it partially rot, before burying it with a mix of sand and animal manure.

Young was one of the very few to report on a Bargy tradition where boys and fishermen went to Newfoundland in May, coming back in October. They journeyed on English boats which visited Waterford, to the west of Bargy, to pick up crews. There was a long tradition of going to eastern Canada for the lucrative fishing season. It was expensive to be taken to Newfoundland, the trip out cost a Yole £3 in late 1770's money, the trip back cost £1.10 Shillings, but the rewards for a tough dangerous few months' work were huge, £15 to £24, very large money for that era.

The people are uncommonly industrious and a most quiet race. There is no such thing as robbery the small farmers live very comfortably and are happy many of them are worth several hundred Pounds.

They are exceedingly attentive in getting mould out of ditches and banks, they mix a little dung with it and then spread it out on the land. They are always on the watch for seaweed and when the tide comes in, even in the middle of the night, they go out in their boats and pick all they can.

They all speak a broken Saxon language and not one in a hundred knows any Irish. They are evidently a distinct people, their features and cast of countenance vary very much from the common native Irish. The girls and women are handsomer having much better features and complexions. Their industry is superior to their neighbours. Along the coast there is a considerable fishery for herrings, every little creek has four or five boats, they sell their herrings to merchants from Wexford, who barrel them for the West Indies.

Both men and women wear straw hats.

Another visitor in 1780, **General Vallancey**

When I was first acquainted with this colony a few of both sexes wore the ancient dress, that of a man was of a short coat, waistcoat and trunk breeches, with a round hat and narrow brim. That of the woman was a short jacket, a petticoat bordered at the rim with one, two, or three riband or tapes of a different colour. The dress of the head was a kircher.

The people of this area live well, are industrious, clean, and of good morals, the poorest farmer eats meat twice a week, and the table of a wealthy farmer is daily furnished with beef, mutton, or fowl, the beverage is home brewed ale or beer, of an excellent colour and flavour.

The houses of the poorest are well built and well thatched, all have out-offices for cattle, fowl, carts, and cars. The people are well clothed, strong, and laborious. The women do all manner of rustic work, ploughing excepted, they receive equal wages with the men.

Fuel is scarce, the chief firing is furze, planted on the tops of all the dykes. These are cut and dried and bring a good return.

E.M. Forster visiting in 1847

At this time it is difficult to see any marked difference between the appearance of the country or the people and England and its population. They are of the same cleanliness, order, and neatness. Great industry exists among a peaceable and well-disposed people. The houses are clean swept and whitewashed, the pig is where it ought to be, in its stye in the yard.

Visitors like Forster were increasingly painting Forth and Bargy as a little industrious part of England, quite different to the rest of Ireland. Forth and Bargy combined are about the same size as a small English county, transplanted into the southeastern tip of Ireland. Visitors got the impression that Forth and Bargy were part of the English Empire, and not part of Ireland.

This author is not to be confused with the English novelist, E.M. Foster, who lived much later, and died in 1970.

Dr. George Hadden

Dr. Hadden (1882-1973) was a Wexford historian who founded the Old Wexford Society in 1944, now titled the Wexford Historical Society.

Figure 12 Photo from the Journal of Wexford Historical Society. Dr George Hadden, the veteran Wexford historian wrote extensively about Yola.

In its Journal in 1970 he wrote the following:

The Baronies where time stood still

One unforeseen result of the isolation of the Baronies was the evolution there of a language unique within their borders.

The first mention of it appears in Standihurst's, Description of Ireland, Standihurst writes, the most Southern part of the county, as the most civil part is contained within a river called the Pill, where the auncientest gentlemen descended from the first conquerors do inhabit.

These gentlemen were doubtless descended from the displaced gentry of estates overrun by Art McMurrow Kavanagh in 1406, who had found sanctuary in this folk settled area of the South.

Holinshead in his Chronicles, discussing the survival of the English language in the Pale, and still apparently quoting Standihurst, wrote,

But of all other places Weisfiord, in the territorie bayed and perclosed within the river called the Pill, was quite so extranged from Irishry that if any traveller of the Irish had pitched his foot within the Pill and spoken Irish, the Weisfordians would command him to turn the other end of his tongue and speake English, or else to bring his trenchmen with him.

Origin of Yola according to Dr Hadden

But Standihurst had already noted the existence of the dialect and offers his own explanation of it. Standihurst wrote, but in our day they have so aquainted themselves with the Irish that they have made a minglemagle or gallimafreie of both languages and commonlie the inhabitants of the meaner sort speak neither good English nor good Irish.

It may question as to whether Standihurst had himself any knowledge of Irish, Hadden points out. The content of Irish in the dialect appears actually to be small, Hadden adds.

Dr Hadden's two other theories as to the origin of Yola:

An alternative theory is that the dialect branched off from the mainstream of English speech at Chaucer, who was actually writing at the time when the building of the Taghmon Line was isolating the Baronies. Something of this sort may have been at the back of Sir Henry Wallop's comment in 1581 when Wallops wrote,

To this day they generally speak ould English.

But back to Hadden, he wrote:

> A third conjecture is that the dialect evolved from the Babel of speech in the folk settlement after the Norman invasion. Standihurst's dialect speakers of the meaner sort would then have been descendents of the rank and file colonists, uninfluenced by the Chaucerian and Shakespearian English of the refugee gentry from the North. But neither has a search for supposed Flemish elements in the dialect yielded much.

The fading out of the dialect according to Hadden.

> Throughout the centuries these baronies on the coastal enclave, lived for the most part in peace, intermarrying strictly within theirin in their own community, retaining their own customs, and most characteristically of all, speaking their own ancient language.
>
> Change was slow. In 1536 Parliament took the first step by resuming the bankrupt palatinate lordship into the King's hands .This basically strengthened the whole County administration. In the more stable conditions that ensued after the tragic chaos of the 1600's, together

with the slow passing of the medieval way of life conditions became more like those we are accustomed to.

Defended tower houses gave way to open, wide windowed mansions, the Taghmon barrier ceased to have any meaning, and the road veto of 1453 gave place to the Grand Jury roads that so impressed Arthur Young in the 1750's. In 1759 Aymer de Valence's Fortress Wexford was declared an open town and its gates dismantled.

As the isolation was relaxed, the use of the dialect waned. Writing in 1867 Rev. D. Webb recorded that already 100 years earlier the dialect had ceased to be spoken in Bargy; but that in the barony of Forth, during the past 40 years the dialect was still the mother tongue of all the residents over 70 years of age.

And so, in this enclave of the Belgic Celts ends this saga of the Norman occupation and decay. Today little but the Walls of Wexford and the ruined towers of the Taghmon Line remain to remind us of so much history.

But in this enclave of the Baronies, the people are uniquely the people of the Isolation.

Hadden's blunt description of the Yoles, above, is most probably true.

Mrs S.C. Hall

Anna Maria Hall (6 January 1800 – 30 January 1881) was a novelist who often published as "Mrs. S. C. Hall".

*Figure 13 from Wikipedia. **Mrs S.C. Hall**, born Dublin, 1800, pictured here five years before she died in 1881.*

She used the initials of her husband, County Waterford born, Stanley Carter Hall, a London literary editor, ditching her own name, Ann, or Anna Fielding, it is not clear why she and her mother moved to England.

Modern history has not been kind to Mrs Hall, the academic, Terence Browne of Trinity College Dublin, recently described her as "a bad writer", not everyone agrees. Also, Browne is writing from the present day, it must have been difficult for an Irish writer in Victorian Britain, for a woman who punched Irish, Yola, and Bannow words, into her books. She must have been persuasive to get her English publisher to accept these words. The English and Scottish reading public loved her works, and with her books on travels in Ireland, she became a unique one-person promoter of Ireland as a travel destination, just when reliable timed ferries and an Irish train system emerged in the mid to last quarter of the 19th century when package holidays were born.

She also wrote that it was less expensive to holiday in Ireland that the rest of Europe.

History again, in modern times, is not kind to Stanley Carter Hall, Stanley and his wife had been friendly with Charles Dickens, but they had a sad falling out and the ever-bitter Dickens nastily portrayed Stanley as an architect villain in one of his lesser-known novels.

Dickens and the Carter Halls never made up.

Figure 14 from Wikipedia. Charles Dickens was a friend of the Bannow writer, Mrs. S.C. Hall, and her editor husband, Stanley Carter Hall, however their friendship ended badly.

Mrs S.C. Hall had a prolific literary output, books mainly, fiction and travel, but also plays, and short stories. She combined with her husband Stanley, in some books about their travels to Ireland, somewhat preachy, taking the line that England was a superior place and that Ireland should learn from its great neighbour. She was also over enthralled with landlords in Ireland, relying on them to bring about social change, she ignored widespread land agitation, and the spirit of revolution in the 19th century. There was hardly a decade in that era when an anti-English revolution was not plotted, or tried, yet she ignored all that. She barely recognised the Famine of the 1840's and argued that somehow the "noble landlords" would fix everything.

All of the above said, Mrs Hall loved Yola, Irish words, and the Bannow dialect, at a time when, in England, there was a 19th century hostility to everything Irish, including the Irish language, the latter referred to negatively by Fleet Street, one report suggested that spoken Irish sounded like "the barking of dogs".

Mrs Hall and her husband visited Ballytrent in coastal Forth, and she wrote of the old tradition, centuries earlier, of Sun God adoration in that area, a line that took considerable courage, and must have enraged much of the Victorian Christian tradition.

Ballytrent was the very spot where the editor, Edmund Hore, had hosted, the Lord Lieutenant, the Earl of Musgrave, to Yolas last gasp in 1836.

It has not been explained why Hore choose Ballytrent as the site of Yola's last hurrah, before railways and motor cars were about, in 1836 it was a difficult place to reach for his farewell kiss to his beloved Yola dialect, knowing it was doomed. Ballytrent most probably had Yola speakers, given its remoteness, and Hore may have wanted listeners capable of understanding his speech, reproduced in Yola and English from page 85.

Ballytrent lies a few miles south of what is known today as Rosslare Europort and is a remote spot today.

Mrs Hall has left us some excellent Victorian travel writings of Ireland and some fine illustrations, including her native Bannow, and Ferrycarrig outside Wexford.

Jacob Poole

Jacob Poole was a Quaker farmer and antiquarian, born in 1774, into a large landowning family near Taghmon, in Forth. As a young man, he grew up on other family owned land four miles south of Wexford. In 1795 he was shocked to see Catholics on their knees out in the cold, the overflow from Sunday Mass, in a tiny shack. He was so moved by the Catholics misery that the next day he donated land for the building of a new Catholic church and gave a generous donation to start fundraising for the start of that new church. That was highly unusual for a person of one religion to donate to another, it would be unusual in Ireland today. Ruins of that church, at Kilmacree, are visible today.

Poole is central to this book, without him we would know little of Yola. An antiquarian in a different era when a considerable chunk of the population were illiterate and barefoot. Poole took an interest in quite a spectrum of areas, including the birds of Wexford harbour, botany, and military matters, he was also interested in the local dialect, Yola spoken by his tenants, and his staff.

He collected a 1700 Glossary, words, and songs, according to the Taghmon Historical society, it was eventually published in Dublin and London in 1867, 40 years after Poole's death. These were surely brave publishers to bring out a book on such a minority topic, a dialect only spoken in remote south-east county Wexford, in an era when literacy levels were quite low.

In poor health with rheumatism in the latter part of his life, he attended the Richmond Hospital in Dublin, in a medical era when little could be done to alleviate his suffering. He died in Taghmon, on the family farm, and is buried in the Quaker graveyard at Forest nearby, his grave is now overgrown.

Rev. William Barnes

The Reverend William Barnes was seemingly an expert on the grammar of the Dorsetshire dialect and was drafted in to edit Poole's Glossary. Barnes seemingly made some mistakes, University College Dublin, scholars suggest. The following pages show what he wrote about Yola pronunciation. The "Mr. Hore" he quotes is probably the Wexford historian, who wrote the multi volume, *Hores History of Wexford*, and not, Edward Hore, the editor of the Wexford Independent, a writer and speaker of Yola.

NOTES ON THE PRONUNCIATION OF FORTH ENGLISH

By WILLIAM BARNES

Mr Hore writes that to give any idea of the Forth dialect one must speak slowly, 'that the letter *a* has invariably the same sound, like *a* in father. Double *ee* sounds like *e* in me; and in most words of two syllables the long accent is placed on the last. To follow the English pronunciation completely deprives the dialect of its peculiarities.'

We are not told what was the sound of the single *e*, or *y*, or long *i*, nor of the diphthongs.

Eight sounds meet us in English grammar.

1. *ee* in meet.
2. *e* long, Dorset.
3. *a* in mate.
4. *ea* in earth, or the French *e* in le.
5. *a* in father.
6. *aw* in awe.
7. *o* in rope.
8. *oo* in food.

Besides diphthongs of pairs of these sounds.

The English 3rd sound long seems to have been in Forth the 5th sound written *aa*, or a sound written with *au*, whether it was the 5th or 6th, as

| F. | aake, | faace, | faade, | glaade, | laace, | maake. |
| E. | ache, | face, | fade, | glade, | lace, | make. |

| F. | naume, | taale, | gaume. |
| E. | name, | tale, | game. |

Our double letters *ai* are often y, as

| F. | agyne, | amyne, | bryne, | gryne, | gry, | pyle, | ryne. |
| E. | again, | amain, | brain, | grain, | gray, | pail, | rain. |

| F. | mye, | mydhe. |
| E. | may, | maid. |

In other cases our *ai* are a diphthong *aay*, as

| F. | daaily, | faigh, | gaay, | haail, | laay, | paay, | waaite. |
| E. | daily, | faith, | gay, | hail, | lay, | pay, | wait. |

answering to the Dorset *aï*,

faïth, gaÿ, haïl, paÿ, waït.

Our *and* of the 5th sound are often shown as *oan* of the 7th sound, or a diphthong of the 7th and a closer sound, sometimes written *one* or *oan*.

F. {brone,	eelone,	hone,	lone,	sthone,	sthrone.
broan,	eeloan,	hoan,	loan,	sthoan,	sthroan.
E. brand,	island,	hand,	land,	stand,	strand.

The 7th or 4th short-sounded *u* is often *ou*.

| F. | chourch, | chourle, | gooun, | spourr, | jooudge. |
| E. | church, | churl, | gun, | spur, | judge. |

In some words *i*, as

| F. | rin, | risheen. |
| E. | run, | rushing. |

Figure 15 Rev Barnes' notes on Yola

52

Our long *i* diphthong of the 4th and 1st, as in *bride*, is mostly represented by *ee* or *ie* 1st.

F.	E.		F.	E.
griende,	grind.		neeght,	night.
heegh,	high.		ree,	rye.
neeghe,	nigh.		skee,	sky.
neen,	nine.		threeve,	thrive.
peepeare,	piper.			

Our diphthong *ou*, *ow*, has mostly become the pretty *eou* which we sometimes hear from London or Eastern County lips, as

F.	greound,	keow,	meouth,	pleough,	sneow,	steout.
E.	ground,	cow,	mouth,	plough,	snow,	stout.

A knowledge of these voicings of the speech will afford us some guidance for the correction of the unsettled spelling of the Glossary, by the bringing of an ill-grounded and almost single form of spelling to the better grounded form of the more usual shape.

The Forth shows a softening of the *f* into *v*, and the *s* into *z*.

It may have been in these clippings (articulations) that some readers may have deemed that they had found in the Forth dialect a mark of the Flemish; but it so happens that they are no more Flemish than they are West English, since, in Somerset and Dorset, they are yet strong, and in the Forth dialect they are coupled with another likeness to Wessex speech, the use of the affix to the past participle, which in Old English was written *y*, in Dorset is *a*, as the French *e* in *le*, and in Forth *ee*, as

F.	ee-sarith	uth in cooanes.
D.	a-sarrd	out in (wooden) cans.
F.	platheares	ee-zet in a row.
D.	platters	a-zet in a row.
F.	Ho ro !	mee cuck is ee-go.
D.	Ho ro !	my cock is a-gone.

The likeness of the Forth and Dorset dialects may be shown by the numerals, as

F.	D.		F.	D.
oan,	one.		zeese,	zix.
twye, } twyne, }	two		zeven,	zeven.
dhree,	dree.		ayght,	aïght.
voure,	vower.		neen,	nine.
veeve,	vive.		dhen,	ten.

Two consonants are sometimes parted by a voicing, as in the *vistes* and *postes* of Wessex,

halef,	half.	calef,	calf.

The more common plural ending is *es*, which, as Dr Russell has observed, and as it seems from the measure of some of the verses, goes on to the singular word not only with its clipping *s*, as in English, but as a full-breath sound, as

'dugg-es an kaud-es,' dogs and cats.

Figure 16 Rev Barnes' notes on Yola (part 2)

53

Some nouns, however, are found with the old Friesic-English plural ending *en*, as Ashen, ashes; Been, bees; Eeen, Ein, eyes; Fleen, fleas; Kyne, cows; Pizzen, peas; Shoone, shoes; Toan, toes; Tren, trees.

Another likeness of Forth to West English is the form of the pronoun *ich, I,* and its blending as *'ch* with verbs.

'Cham, for Ich aam, I am.
'Chas, for Ich waas, I was.
'Cha, for Ich ha, I have.
'Chull, for Ich wull, I will.
'Chood, for Ich would, I would.

In Devon we find,

'Cham, I am.
'Chave, I have.
'Chad, I had.
'Chell, I will or shall.
'Chant, I won't or shan't.

'May be chell and may be chant,' for, 'It may be I shall, and it may be I shall not.'

The definite article of the older Forth was *a* or *ee.*

There are a few markworthy cases of the softening of our *p* into a *b,* and of *t* into *d,* as in blenty, for plenty; boor, for poor; dell, for till; Beedher, for Peter, but this might have slipped in from the change of clipping in Irish.

Figure 17 Rev Barnes' notes on Yola (part 3)

Yola land leases

Leases lasted one to 20 years, or in some cases 35 years, with the landlord very much in control, if the tenant improved his cabin the landlord looked for a higher rent.

In 1776, a cottage with one acre in Bargy fetched a rent of £3 yearly.

Rents varied considerably, some were expensive, others quite modest, there are reports of landlords leaving the rent unchanged for 30 years. Visitors to Forth and Bargy repeatedly refer to neat cottages, better than the rest of Ireland. Nonetheless, in 1841, a third of all tenants in Forth and Bargy lived in one-roomed mud cabins, the photo reproduced in Figure 4 gives us some idea of the impoverished life these people lived.

The lease was usually left to the eldest son.

In some arrangements, a poor farmer and his children worked part-time for a landlord, payment was small and was partially in food and fuel. The tenant and his family worked for two days during sowing time, and another two days during harvesting, and a third stint of two days hoeing, they were most probably badly paid, or not paid, for this work.

Figure 18 from a painting by Frank Mckelvey, from Whyte's the Dublin art dealers catalogue

Landlords rented out around three quarters of their estates in leases that lasted up to 30 years.

invader landlords got farms of 600 to 700 acres, substantial holdings, they kept one third for their own use, and rented out the balance. Some reports suggest Yola landlords had holdings of up to 900 acres, but 700 acres is probably more accurate. Landlords were fairly wealthy, living first in castles and later in fine wide mansions, also called Big Houses and tended to dominate their tenants.

Figure 19 taken with permission from a Parish and its People

Compared with the rest of Ireland, landlord and tenant relations were good.

Yoles as fishermen and fowlers

While most of the Yoles were independent farmers, providing all their own food, clothes, and shoes, some were hunter-gatherers, fishing, harvesting shellfish, and killing wildfowl, rabbits, and hares.

Herring, cod, lobster, and oysters, were the main target of sea fishing in small boats, much of it nocturnal, lucrative but dangerous, and hard work, and disappointing when herring shoals did not materialise, from time to time after 1830. That proved to be a disaster for full-time fishermen, who

56

then had to rely on charity. There was an earlier herring boom in Wexford around 1654, some 80,000 barrels of herring were landed with another 40,000 barrels likely landed, but not registered probably for tax reasons. But by 1682 this boom had ended. But the herring fishing continued over the centuries, with barrels of herring exported to England as regular sea links emerged, and in barrels to the West Indies.

Figure 20 from a drawing by Markey Robinson, Whyte's Dublin art dealers catalogue. Women did not go fishing on the boats, there were no toilets.

Yola women did not go sea fishing, but they did collect shellfish.

The herring fishermen off Forth and Bargy developed their own superstitions, including refusing to fish on certain nights, such as the Eve of St. Martins night. Some fishermen who defied this traditional ban were drowned, and their deaths are recorded in a grim ballad.

Meeting a woman on their way to the boat was an omen of bad luck, all the more so if she was barefoot or had red hair. Some fishermen turned back home had they met a woman or seen a hare. Three men of the same surname could not fish out of the same boat. Smoking, *smockeen,* in the boat, was not allowed.

In conversation aboard the fishing cot, the word priest was avoided, instead, they talked of "the man with the collar".

For good luck fishermen's families threw a hot coal after them as they left the house to go fishing. Boats were decorated with green sprigs tied to the mast or fishermen's clothes. On St. Brigid's Day fishermen placed empty seashells in the four corners of their homes to bring them good luck.

Fishermen would not allow fish bones to be thrown on the fire.

The Rosary was said in the boat at midnight.

In the Faythe area of Wexford households made and repaired fishing nets.

At that time small Wexford ports like Bannow boomed, with as many as 30 ships visiting and providing passenger access to Dublin and ports in England.

Figure 21 painting from St, Peters College, Wexford. This old painting dates from 1820 and shows the Deep Pool, now the Crescent, on the Wexford seafront.

Herrings were hunted along the Wexford coast in cots, the traditional boats of Wexford Harbour. Along the coast, a larger cot, with several masts, was developed, such as the Rosslare cot, with higher sides than those used on the river Slaney. Where there was no inlet, these cots were launched off beaches, using rollers, and again landed with rollers, tough work hauling a cot up onto a beach. A fleet of 100 boats worked off the beach at Tachumshane, with a similarly sized fleet in Kilmore Quay, and a smaller fleet in Bannow. While herring fishing was dangerous and tough work, like Yola farming, it changed little over the centuries and was exceptionally well paid.

Around 1910 a herring fishing cot would earn £300-£3,000 per boat for a six-week season, very good money split between two or three men. Herring fishermen from Rosslare developed heavy drinking habits out of their huge earnings, then again £3,000 for six weeks work was largely unheard of in Ireland at that time.

The higher earning Rosslare herring cots were likely to have been large, 40-foot boats, with three masts, probably with a crew of six.

That £3,000 figure is extraordinarily high and may well be a wild exaggeration, suffice it to say that the herring season yielded high payment for its fishermen.

Figure 22 from a print by Markey Robinson, from Whyte's, Dublin art auctioneers, portrays fishermen drinking after a catch

Heavy drinking ensued after the close of the herring season in Rosslare, and nearby inland in Kilrane, with fishermen drinking all night into morning, and publicans only too keen to illegally stay open to trap this booming trade. Inevitably, fishermen and publicans were before the courts caught by the police for drinking during illicit hours.

Judges were lenient in their decisions over such cases.

The Yoles fished eels in rivers and lakes and kept eel skin utilising it the making of trashers. Eels were speared using a four-pronged spear, with a handle furthest from the barbs, a short rope was attached to the handle. Spears were relatively inexpensive items, produced by blacksmiths. Eels were also caught with lines and bobs.

Several species of shellfish were harvested including oysters, cockles, clams, mussels, periwinkles, and barnacles. Around Bannow cockles were harvested mainly from May to August, they were eaten in hot milk, or buttermilk, on Wednesdays and Fridays. Cockle pickers worked up until midnight on Thursdays, then loaded their harvest onto carts and set out for New Ross getting to that town early on Friday morning. Other pickers used a former ferry from Ballyhack to bring their cargo westwards to Waterford, and there were fishmongers known as "the Taghmon jolters" who also bought their catch.

Seemingly barnacles were eaten in another era, it is unclear whether anyone in south Wexford eats this species today, but the Irish Examiner newspaper recently reported that barnacles are still eaten in Cork but in a very small way. A Cork girl who eats barnacles was introduced to them by her Grandfather, who hailed from the Canary Islands. The barnacles are cut off rocks with a knife, then cooked.

In a Yola house cockles were spread on a cloth in the centre of a table and eaten with potatoes. They are, of course, a delicacy in Spain and Portugal today.

Mussels taken off rocks have been eaten in the coastal area of Forth and Bargy for centuries and are widely eaten today. Very small amounts of clams, periwinkles, and limpets are eaten today, generally, by people who pick them off rocks or pools, they are not sold in shops, or served in pubs or restaurants. The main pickers of these species today seem to be marine scientists, and fish processors, and their families.

A limpet is called a *barnaugh* in Yola, limpets are also called *Bring-awns* in Yola.

Oysters were harvested in Wexford harbour over the centuries, widely eaten in the town, and its taverns, yielding the name, Oyster Lane, off South Main Street. It seems oyster stocks in Wexford harbour were largely exhausted by the end of 20th century. An attempt to reseed and restart this industry in the 21st century has hit serious problems, a harvesting permit is essential from the Government, but the health authorities are opposed to oyster farming in Wexford Harbour, the future of a hoped-for revival in oyster fishing in that Harbour looks uncertain.

Landlords transplanted oysters from Milford Haven, in Wales, and successfully grew them in Bannow at the western edge of Bargy. The Bannow oysters are described as larger than Milford Haven oysters.

Over the centuries a tradition of small-scale smuggling developed along the south Wexford coast, it continues today.

The Yoles hunted rabbits and hares, both were part of their food, snares were used to trap rabbits. They were plenty of these small animals on the very flat land of Forth and Bargy, particularly around Kilmore, Kilmore Quay, and Tomhaggard.

There was a superstition among the Yoles that it was bad luck to see a hare sitting on a fence. Another bit of bad luck was said to attach to a person who put on their left sock ahead of the right.

Brat seems to be an old English word, and refers to the cooking of fish, such as turbot, on an open fire. Whether *Brat* made its way into Yola is unclear.

The Yoles were also fowlers, such as those who lived on the Rosslare Fort up into the 20th century where Yola was seemingly last spoken. We do not have a death of the dialect date, it had been suggested it was the late 1920s but quite recently the 1970s seems more likely. It now seems there is at least one writer of Yola, alive in 2018, he can speak a little of the dialect. He lives in Galway.

The Fort bird hunters caught fowl, about a dozen bird types, on the Rosslare side of Wexford harbour and sold their catch in Wexford, delivered by boat, such was the isolation of the Rosslare Fort, seemingly one of the most remote villages in County Wexford, if not the entire country.

The Yoles also speared fish, using a traditional short eel-spear attached to a rope of a few feet long, that spearing tradition continued into the 1960's, young men from Wexford used to climb down into the timber beams of a Slaney bridge, now demolished, near the Wexford Boat Club, at Carcur, and speared fish.

More often they speared eels, mullet, or bass, but if they got lucky, they speared a valuable salmon.

The spearing tradition died out when that bridge was demolished in the 1960's.

After the Famine in 1840's, there was renewed interest in all types of fishing in Forth and Bargy, but these two baronies were not as badly hit by the potato blight as elsewhere in Ireland.

Yola Traditions

Funeral Cross tradition in South Wexford

The Yoles had their traditions, including a funeral tradition of laying a cross on a bush near a graveyard, it survives only in Kilmore, together with Yola based Christmas carols, also sung nearby in Kilmore Quay, three miles away. The leaving of a cross on a bush or hawthorn tree was common in south-east Wexford in times past. Originally, the crosses were made out of spare timber by the coffin maker, in the era when a coffin was made by a local carpenter. The crosses measured about two feet from top to base, while the horizontal piece was about 11 inches wide.

Figure 23 drawing from the Journal of the Royal Society of Antiquities of Ireland. For centuries there was a funeral tradition in Forth and Bargy, mourners carried timber crosses deposit deposited in a tree at the graveyard, ably drawn by the artist, George du Noyer, employed by the old British Civil Service in Dublin, to draw Irish antiquities in Ireland. This tradition continues today only in Kilmore.

The mourners carried crosses, one was spear shaped at the base, this cross was placed on the coffin before the procession started, when the coffin was in the ground this cross was driven into the soil at the head of the grave, it remained in place until a headstone was erected, or was left to rot if there was not a headstone.

The other crosses were placed by mourners in a tree, often hawthorn, or a bush.

Over time the tree or bush got weighed down with crosses, in Kilmore the crosses are now in a roadside heap at Brandycross. Years ago, the crosses were brightly painted, today they are either varnished or unpainted. It is suggested that the funeral cross tradition originated in Germany, France, and the Basque region of Spain, and the tradition made its way to the West of England via pilgrims and little-known saints. Poor rural people in mainland Europe were given to myths and took to meeting at crossroads late on Christmas and New Year's Eve, they hoped to hear voices that would forecast how they would fare over the coming year. It was these people who used the funeral cross tradition. That tradition of funeral crosses is specifically mentioned in Somersetshire by Margaret Stokes, writing in the Journal of the Royal Society of Antiquities in Ireland, in 1894. Then the Yoles brought the cross tradition to County Wexford.

Irish pilgrims, quite separate to the Yoles, brought the wooden cross funeral tradition to Cong, in County Mayo, the same Margaret Stokes mentioned above, recorded the Cong tradition, seemingly now dead. Stokes did not record such a tradition elsewhere in Ireland, so it now seems to survive only in Kilmore. The Yoles had no connection with Cong.

The Cong wooden cross funeral tradition could have been started by St. Fursa, a little-known Mayo saint who worked for a time in England.

Figure 24 This painting of the Catholic Mass tradition in a mud cabin 1883 is by Aloysius O Kelly (1853-1936) from the National Gallery of Ireland

The funeral wooden cross tradition was common in Forth and Bargy, heaps of crosses could be seen in the 19th century, including those at Tenacre, near Rosslare, Kilturk, Bannow, and Tomhaggard. A vertical line divides Forth from Bargy through, starting at the Forth mountain then stretching south to Tomhaggard then down to the Atlantic on the south coast.

Kilmore Carols

A striking old church music tradition continues in south Wexford, in Kilmore village at Christmas, when 300-year-old carols are sung in Yola, unlike any village in Ireland. These carols are sung by six men split into two groups, singing verses in turn, there are no female singers. The carols, one from 16th century English, in ye olde English, are passed down in families, or at work, and always to this day, singers include a Devereux, pronounced in Kilmore by some with an x at the end of the name.

These thirteen carols are sung very slowly, with the words distinctly eased out, in a Yola style drawl.

Over the decades the Kilmore carol singers have had to battle with priests who tried to move or banish them, their carol is always sung during the Consecration of the Mass, efforts by bullying priests to move them from that slot, failed.

The carols, as apart from the English one, were composed by a bishop and priest, both known, and contain significant Yola words.

In recent years a team of music staff, from University College Cork, tried to modernise the Kilmore carols, depending on who you talk to, this worked/did not work, - but it's the old carols that will likely be sung in Kilmore this Christmas.

It is remarkable that the main continuance of Yola traditions are both focused on Kilmore, the southern edge of Forth, its burial cross tradition, and its magnificent Christmas carols.

Yola continues in some small ways in Kilmore to these days. Yola is often the name given to a boat. There is a boat called Yola today on Kilmore Quay. Some girls in Forth and the diaspora are named Yola.

Yola dance tradition

There was a dawn dancing tradition among the Yoles, on St. Johns Eve near the longest day of summer, young people met on commonage, or shared land. They lit a bonfire at dusk and kept it alight until dawn, fiddles and pipes provided the music, girls gathered in a circle, holding hands around the fire, and danced clockwise. Boys gathered in an outer circle and danced anti-clockwise. As the fire went down couples, holding each other, jumped over the fire, and later danced through the ashes. This dance tradition lasted up into the third quarter of the 19th century. It was celebrated in Cromwell's Fort in Wexford, but eventually drew the wrath of priests who engineered the demise of the Johns Eve dusk to dawn dance.

The Yoles had many other dusk to dawn dances, some on various feast days, and farmers threw parties for their harvest workers, which continued into all night dancing.

Yola weddings

Yola weddings involved all night dancing, body contact seemingly got out of hand, historians have disclosed few details about this, but Yola weddings were wild celebrations, some reports suggest these weddings were promiscuous.

The bride sat at the head of a table and when she danced her chair was taken by a bridesmaid. The wedding guests cut up apples into small pieces and pelted or threw the pieces at each other. Girls married around 14 plus, boys in their late teens, couples usually lived together before marriage, a tradition at variance with their neighbours, where, we are told, a Catholic Irish virgin tradition persisted.

Figure 25 from the National Gallery of Ireland, artist David Teniers

Above depicts a wedding scene in the mid-1640's giving us an idea how people dressed and danced, by David Teniers. Though Flemish, it gives us a hint of what a Yola wedding celebration would have looked like.

Figure 26 from the National Gallery of Ireland, Daniel Maclise 1854

This painting by Daniel Maclise is of the original Yola wedding, when Strongbow, a Norman invader, married Aoife, the daughter of an Irish King, painting dated 1854.

Yola Songs or Zongs

While some Yola songs survive the musical scores are lost. What we have today are poems, it is up to singers to improvise old Irish airs. If you look to YouTube, you will see county Wexford man, Paddy Berry, doing this very well. In 1969, RTE, the Irish state TV company, made a programme on Yola, it was presented by the late linguist, Diarmaid O'Muirithe, and it was seemingly his idea to include a Yola song. He approached Berry who sings in Yola, to an old Irish air, an excellent performance. Berry, from Bargy, sings, composes, and publishes music.

Figure 27 photo from RTE. Pictured in the white sweater, from 1969, is Paddy Berry, singing a traditional Yola song, which can be viewed on YouTube.

This is the same Diarmaid O'Muirithe, who together with T.P. Dolan, newly edited, Poole's Glossary in 1979, a brilliant work. Poole was a considerable collector of Yola songs, they are included in his Glossary, or Dictionary, alas without the music.

Other Yola songs are appearing in Wikipedia, such as "The Maiden of Rosslare".

In Yola	In English
Ee mydhe ov Rosslaar	The Maiden of Rosslare
Cham goen to tell thee oo tale at is drue	I'm going to tell you a tale that is true

The rest of this song can be viewed on Wikipedia, together with another, titled "An Old Yola song", which also appears in Poole's Glossary, is a considerable 14 verse song.

There are other Yola songs including "The Weddeen of Ballymore", collected by Poole from Lett Sealy, one of his tenants, in 1823.

There is another song titled, "Verses in Answer to the Wedding of Ballymore", said to have been written by a Catholic priest named Devereux.

"The Brides Portion" is another Yola song, as is "Patrick Codd's Lamentation", also called, "Castle Codd's Lamentation".

Another Yola song is titled, "About An Old Sow Going To Be Killed".

"Zong of twi maaakeet moans" is another Yola song, translated into "Song of two market women".

For now, Paddy Berry on YouTube is the best we can view.

The Dublin traditional music archivist, Nicholas Carolan, has posted material about Yola on YouTube, he describes the dialect as a mix of several languages from the many invaders into south-east Wexford. Carolan's description is probably accurate, he has also posted footage of Paddy Berry's excellent singing.

Figure 28 from the National Gallery of Ireland

As for musical instruments when the Normans invaded the Irish only had harps and small hand-beaten drums called timpanums, better known today as tambourines. The invaders introduced uileann pipes in the 12th century, depicted above in 1841 by artist Patrick Haverty.

Wexford Carol

Now for another tale; William Grattan Flood (1859-1928) was an organist and chorister in St. Aidan's Cathedral, in Enniscorthy, he heard there was an undocumented carol, known as "The Wexford Carol" said to date from the 12th century, the hint being that it might be part of the Yola tradition. He duly recorded that carol, it was said to be sung by men only, which tied in with the Yola male dominant tradition. This carol is also known by its first line "Good People All This Christmas Day". Grattan Flood did not push a Yola connection.

The music industry and various performers very successfully pushed this 12th century line, but it now has been debunked, the Wexford carol is more likely to date from the 16th century or 18th. That is the verdict from music academics today. There is a dispute whether this carol was originally written in English or Irish, it is also known as "The Enniscorthy Carol".

As with many old songs, there is a continuing debate about the origin and longevity of this carol, it probably evolved over the centuries, and may well have been originally composed in Irish.

Banging of the Door property transfer tradition

This is a little-known tradition, alive until recently, if not alive today.

Seemingly it applies to a commercial property, like a pub or shop. The selling publican invited his customers in for a last free drink, and the purchasing publican was introduced.

After the customers had had their final free drinks, the seller produced the front door key, after inserting it in the lock, he slowly banged the door closed three times, before handing the key to the new owner, to loud applause.

This ceremony usually happened at lunchtime, if a stranger was by chance in that pub, he was invited to join in the festivity and given a free drink.

The banging-of-the-door tradition was alive 40 years ago and may well be discreetly alive today. Discretion is a Yola trait.

Drinkings Party

Only in very recent years have we heard of a scenario where the wife of an Irish landlord hosted "a drinkings party" a drinks party confined to *meyen* or women guests. Such parties were not specific to Yoles, and were held by the wives of Irish landlords, but were also likely hosted by Yola landlord wives. They were the brewers and distillers in the household, and by all accounts relationships between Yola landlord wives and their tenants were good.

Figure 29 by George Russell from Whyte's art catalogue

The Landladies also played a pivotal role in selling tenant household produce like clothes, blankets, and cheese.

Some Yola landlord wives organised womens co-ops, with women tenants coming together to make clothes, and clothing materials, the landlord's wife was often the salesperson for the produce.

The same scenario seems to have also applied to cheese making done on farms, but the landlords wife seemingly had a role in co-op sales, involving cheesemongers from Dublin.

Catholic traditions in Forth and Bargy

Until a few decades ago Catholic traditions were quite strong in Forth and Bargy, quite apart from milking cows, very little work was carried out on farms on Sundays, the Lords Day. There was an unspoken ban on "servile work on Sunday ".

Some farms ceased work at noon on Saturday, in deference to Sunday approaching. No farm work was carried out on Sundays, but also on Holy Days, in some places, St. Martins Day, was such a Holy Day, in other places, St. Brigid's Day, was a Holy Day.

In some areas, if a neighbour died during planting, those on nearby farms abandoned their work until after the funeral.

The Rosary was said at midnight on fishing boats, nets were not repaired nor boats painted on Sundays.

Those living in cottages did no external work like liming, or gardening, on the Sabbath, and pubs were closed on that day and Holy days.

While Catholics abstained from meat on Fridays, some of the Yoles went further, and also abstained from meat on Wednesdays, and Saturdays.

Some historians attribute the high number of religious vocations in modern-day Forth and Bargy, to the Yola religious tradition, they include priests, nuns, and brothers and sisters in religious orders, the latter, mainly domestic servants, whose remarkable servile existence is rarely alluded to.

Extreme forms of Catholicism surfaced among the Yoles. In 1824, Rev. John Carroll, a curate in Killinick, in Forth, attempted an exorcism on a four-year-old local girl, Catherine Sinnott. During this religious ritual, with aim of driving demons out, the girl was killed, and Rev. Carroll and five of his parishioners later stood trial for the murder of Catherine Sinnott. Local histories seem to avoid mention of this trial, thus we do not know the verdict. In May 2018 a book giving an account of the trial was offered by book auctioneer, Fonsie Mealy, of Castlecomer. From newspaper reports, the book was seemingly untitled, and there was no mention of an author or publisher, nor was there a mention of a verdict. This text may well have been written by a court stenographer or a policeman.

All this is quite strange, Fr. Carroll and his co-accused may well have been found not guilty, but it is highly unusual for the details of a priest's trial for murdering a four-year-old, not to have made it into local histories.

Figure 30 from the National Gallery of Ireland. Few Irish painters focus on the barefoot Irish yet in 1891, artist Richard Thomas Moynan, did just that with his work, Military Manoeuvres, contrasting the military and the shoeless.

It is argued that the growth of Lady's Island as a place of pilgrimage on August 15th is largely due to the input of the strong Catholic tradition of the Yoles. There are reports of pilgrims from Wexford walking barefoot to Lady's Island on August 15th, returning home barefoot, a round trip of about 12 miles. We forget that in times past quite a chunk of the population was barefoot, and in parts of county Wexford some school children were without shoes up into the 1930's.

The Normans brought their stone carving skills to Forth and Bargy, there is a very good example of their stone carving in the 12th century Norman Font, from Bannow Church, now in Carrig (Figure 8) Harvard University has made a detailed study of the Font, in recent years, and its findings are now lodged with Trinity College Dublin.

Rosslare Fort

The Rosslare Fort was a small village at the mouth of Wexford Harbour - it was initially staffed by soldiers, who in 1649 tried, but failed to stop Cromwell's men from capturing it, before he went on to sack Wexford.

The front and rear cover of this book is from a very old photo of Rosslare taken near the Rosslare Fort where Yola may have been spoken up into the 1920's (from an old postcard, with an English stamp).

THE OLD FORT

Figure 31 Photo from the Centenary Record. This old photo taken from the sea captures the military and colonial aspect of the Fort

For some years the Fort remained derelict, it was occasionally referred to as Clare Fort, but by 1654, it was rebuilt, growing to a peak of 30 families, it had its own school and Catholic church, crucially it had its own well and pump. It had a central square of 12 houses, and a flagstaff, a military design, with guns aimed out to sea, two piers and a frigate moored nearby. The village was built on 740 acres of sand dunes, a high dune called the Hill of Sixty was used as a lookout. Poultry and animals were kept on the Fort, a storm cursed village, (Figure 31) vulnerable to a roaring sea built on sand, unlike other Wexford coastal villages, built on rock. Though connected to Rosslare Strand by a long beach, the village was relatively remote, its residents commuted to Wexford by small timber sailing boats, called cots. This was faster than the long beach trek to Rosslare Strand, for centuries only a crossroads, cum tiny village. The women in the Fort were skilled sailors and could navigate a cot, without their husbands, into the town. There are vivid reports of women from the Fort sailing into Wexford, and when the town flooded, they sailed on the flooded North Main Street!

Who lived on the Fort

A mix of residents lived in Rosslare Fort, soldiers, pilots who guided ships into Wexford, a Life Boat crew, Customs men, Coast Guards, a boat builder, and fishermen, who doubled as fowlers. It is likely that the fishermen cum fowlers were the Yola speakers, their wives dressed Yola style, including aprons called *prankeens*, or praiskeens, yet another of the many Yola words for an apron.

The fowlers developed unique canoe like boats, paddled by hand, and steered by the movement of body weight by the sole occupant, lying face down stretched out, they are still in use today. Called "punt guns" they have a shotgun type gun attached to the bow, and shoot out lead and bits of metal waste, like screws and rivets, quite successfully at wild fowl, as much as 15 types, very much in the hunter gatherer Yola tradition.

Confusingly, several different detailed reports of life on the Rosslare Fort make no mention of Yola or if it was spoken there, it is unexplained, but it is hardly important, when we learn that some Yola was spoken in the bargy of Forth in the 1970 s, and that written Yola rebounded in the form of a prize winning poem in 2018, see Figure 42.

Tough life

The life of the Fort fishermen was a tough one, they were the only people in the village without a salary, and they had to sell their catch in Wexford. They made their own boats, nets, and tackle, and waterproofed knee length sea boots.

Practically everyone else on the Fort were Government employees. With employment, a school, a church opened in 1800, and a water supply, the future for the Rosslare Fort looked good for a time, dances were held at weekends in the band room, part of the British navy property. Young people from Wexford sailed out in a half dozen boats to these dances. They sailed back to Wexford in the dark, a quite difficult dangerous journey with only the lights of the town as a compass, but there are no records of injuries or problems. A priest came from Kilrane, probably by trap or horseback, to say Mass each Sunday. The village was never big enough to support its own priest, while the Protestant grouping on the Fort sailed into Wexford for their service. But by the 1870's activity in this village peaked, half of the 50 houses in the Fort were deserted, by that time Yola was dying elsewhere. The Famine in the 1840's, less wrecking in county Wexford than elsewhere, had accelerated Irish overall emigration, and there was a move from the Fort into towns, where there was a better life.

Some comfortably well-off people also lived on the Fort, in a mix of stone and timber houses, the latter prone to storm damage. Some of the timber houses were rather like the fine two storey quite unusual Irish timber houses, that stand today in the coastal strip of northeast county Wexford, north of Courtown.

The Fort at the turn of the century

Figure 32 Photo from the Book of Kelly's, with permission

After the military withdrew the head Customs man was given the role of Commander of the Fort, the big guns could only be fired on his say so.

Some extraordinary people lived on the Fort including, Ned Wickam, skipper of the Forts Life Boat, he was awarded a silver medal by the King of Norway for his rescue of the crew of the ship Puffin in 1906, he later got a silver clasp from Britain, for his valiant rescue from the Mexico shipwreck on the Keeragh Rocks, off Fethard, in 1914. His Life Boat was towed by a tug from Wexford to offshore Fethard, on the Atlantic, or south coast of the county, and after a three-day battle with a wicked sea, he took a dingy to rescue many men, in the same sea drama when several Fethard Lifeboatmen lost their lives.

Ned Wickam has another place in Wexford history, in 1891 he together with others from the Fort found a beached blue whale near the isolated village. Wickham killed it with a spear, the skeleton, a rarity, was sold to a London museum where it is now on view.

Disaster and drownings

The sea could be cruel to the Fort, such as in 1835, when 11 people attempted to sail home, in a Coast Guard boat, from Wexford. Unfortunately, the crew were drunk, a wild storm ended their voyage, the boat sank, pilots from the Fort, watching the disaster unfold, probably from the Hill of 60, tried to intervene, as did the yacht, G. Morgan. All passengers including women, children, and the crew, drowned, two pigs on board survived, found on nearby sandbanks

Of the dead some were from Protestant families, they are buried close to each other in Kilscoran to the south of Wexford Harbour.

A subsequent enquiry into this disaster confirmed the crew were drunk.

Some of the Forts economy hinged on the Life Boats, it seems that in 1838, a Life Boat station was built in what is described at Rosslare Point, that sounds like near, if not in the Fort, but by 1851, it had lapsed but was restarted in 1858 in the Fort.

For a time, this Life Boat station, - unusually, - had two boats, one afloat, the other beached but ready to launch. The wives of the Life Boat crew helped in the beaching of the Life Boat, by assisting in the turning of a capstan or winch that helped haul the boat off the beach to higher ground.

Good times- wreck cargoes

It was not all bleak news from the Fort, in 1868, 16 cases of rum were found by fishermen off Rosslare, it seems the Fort was also occasionally lucky when deck cargoes washed ashore.

The very isolated location did not help, but that very remoteness probably does explain why Yola may have been spoken there, as the language last survived in distant areas, supposedly dying out elsewhere in Forth in the 1870's, and a century earlier in Bargy, but we don't know when it died out in the Fort. This was the conventional wisdom until 2018.

When the school teacher moved into Wexford, the Fort suffered a serious setback.

For a time, the declining Fort was fashionable with contrastingly comfortably off people from Wexford, who rented or bought some of the empty houses, and used them as holiday accommodation, sailing out in cots, as many as two dozen on Sundays, from Wexford Quay. The weekenders occupied themselves by fishing. There were some very fine stone houses in this village, far more upmarket than in other Wexford villages.

Maritime names move to Rosslare

In the 20th century, the decline of Rosslare Fort accelerated but it was storms that eventually wrecked it, fierce storms in 1924 and 1925 cut it off from Rosslare, the beach was breached, it was then alarmingly, an island, and by 1926, it was deserted, then the wrecked sandy village was quickly reclaimed by the sea. The frightened Fort residents moved into Wexford and Rosslare, the last to leave were pilots, Peter and Larry Furlong, who moved north to the nearby Raven Point, while the Life Boat and its crew moved south to Rosslare. Today all that remains are a few stones, occasionally visible at very low tide. Among the Fort families that moved to Rosslare are the sea faring, Wickams, Duggans, and Walshes, most of them born in the remote, island-like, village.

Among those who moved was Richard Walsh, who was born on the Fort. In Rosslare Harbour he became the skipper of the lifeboat, Douglas Hyde, and in 1954 he showed considerable judgement and bravery in saving the crew of a tanker, Wold Concorde, that had broken into two halves in the Irish Sea.

Ann Shiel of Rosslare, in recent years told the *Wexford People* that her grandparents and great grandparents lived on the Fort. She occasionally visits the watery remains of a now vanished historic Wexford village.

Yola died with the collapse of the Fort, we believed this until 2018.

Figure 33 This painting depicts a typical Irish fishing village by Markey Robinson (from Whytes art catalogue)

Fingalian spoken in north Dublin

This dialect was introduced into the area now known as Fingal county, north of the Tolka river. Like Yola, Fingalian was introduced to this area by Norman invading soldiers. Little of it has survived except for two bawdy poems, and a song, sentences have not survived, except for the poems and there was no Jacob Poole to record it, or newspaper editor to give it a last hurrah. Many Fingalian words survive, and can be found online, while there is other good material about this dialect on YouTube. It faded out in the mid-19th century. While there is very limited enthusiasm for Yola, there is little interest in Fingalian for now, but that could change in time.

The poems were seemingly not written by a Fingalian speaker and take the tone of mocking the dialect.

There are some who argue that Yola and Fingalian share the same roots, but there does not appear to be words that are common to the two dialects.

Online you can view a small collection of words and phrases unique to the Rush and Skerries areas of north county Dublin, but they do not appear to be Fingalian.

We are not told how these words and phrase evolved, nor is there any attempt, in the posting, to link them to Fingalian. There does not seem to be any other invader spawned dialect in the South of Ireland, though Scots Gallic, still alive in a very small way in Northern Ireland, may well have roots similar to Yola. That has yet to be proved.

The Ros Tapestry

The following beautiful images are the creation of the Ros Tapestry, a voluntary group, started in 1998, in New Ross, County Wexford, depicting the early Norman, later to become known as the Yoles. These images are taken from remarkable 15 panels, 6' x 4' on public view in New Ross, a work of 150 local stitchers, telling us about the Normans, set to become the Yoles, *a tale told in thread.* So well said by the stitchers.

Figure 34 The Ros Tapestry. This andd the following images are copyright the Ros Tapestry

The first panel of the selection shows the Normans landing at Bannow, depicting their better horses, and armour, and their colourful regalia. At the bottom edge, we see the Norman hunting dogs, a boat under sail, and a boat tilted down to allow horses to disembark. The journey, of Dermot MacMurragh to visit King Henry 11, in Aquitaine, France, for his approval for the Irish invasion, is also depicted.

Figure 35 The Ros Tapestry, second panel

The second reproduction shows the conquest of Wexford, with the victors looking down into the town from its walls, with the better-armed invaders, Robert Fitzsimons on the right, and his colleague, Dermot MacMurragh, on his left, a lesser armed Leinster King, who organised Fitzsimons "arrogant trespass."

Figure 36 The Ros Tapestry, third panel

The lower panel is remarkable for its detail of a fair in New Ross, dated around 1220, by that time, some 40 years after the invasion, the Normans had made a considerable commercial impact on New Ross, just how they communicated is unclear, perhaps each borrowed phrases from the other's language. This was quite on from the invasion of 1169, and shows Italian bankers, a jester, and hunting dogs. It is unclear whether Yola was spoken in New Ross at that time, but it was likely understood as the language of commerce.

In allowing this author to reproduce their panels, the Ros Tapestry requested that this author would make it clear that the Ros Tapestry does not in any way authenticate or approve this book, the author is glad to mention this.

The Decline of Yola

Wexford newspaper editor gives Yola it's last public outing with the English Viceroy

By 1836 Yola was in fast decline in Forth. In Bargy it was practically dead by 1770, yet Edward Hore the editor of the Wexford Independent, gave it one deathbed boost, inviting the Viceroy, the Earl of Mulgrave, to Ballytrent, in the heart of Forth, below Rosslare, for a speech in Yola which Hore wrote and delivered. He predicted the end of the dialect. The Viceroy, also called the Lord Lieutenant, was England's representative in Ireland, Hore's speech, a rather grovelling short one, was delivered in Yola, with parts in English, the Viceroy probably half slumbered through the editor's talk. Quite a chunk of the audience, listening along with the Viceroy, most probably did not understand the Yola speech, but Hore was giving the dialect its last hurrah. That speech predicted the death of Yola and by 1870 it was largely dead, except perhaps in the Rosslare Fort years later, and then the surprise 2018 development.

Figure 37 Though this painting is Scottish, 1856, it gives us some idea how the Yoles and Irish would appear on St Patricks Day, by Erskine Nicol, (National Gallery of Ireland).

On the following pages are an address in Yola delivered to the Viceroy, the Earl of Musgrave in 1836, in Ballytrent, a speech that was supposed to mark the end of Yola, and following that, an English translation.

Mai't be plesant to th' Eccellencie, — Wee, Vassalès o' 'His Most Gracious Majesty', Wilyame ee Vourthe, an, az wee verilie chote, na coshe an loyale dwellerès na Baronie Forthe, crave na dicke luckie acte t'uck neicher th' Eccellencie, an na plaine garbe o' oure yola talke, wi vengem o' core t'gie oure zense o' ye gradès whilke be ee-dighte wi yer name; and whilke we canna zei, albeit o' 'Governere', 'Statesman', an alike. Yn ercha an aul o' while yt beeth wi gleezom o' core th' oure eyen dwytheth apan ye Vigere o'dicke Zouvereine, Wilyame ee Vourthe, unnere fose fatherlie zwae oure daiez be ee-spant, az avare ye trad dicke londe yer name waz ee-kent var *ee vriene o' livertie*, an *He fo brake ye neckares o' zlaves*. Mang ourzels—var wee dwytheth an Irelonde az ure generale haime—y'ast, bie ractzom o'honde, ee-delt t'ouz ye laas ee-mate var ercha vassale, ne'er dwythen na dicke waie nar dicka. Wee dwyth ye ane fose dais be gien var ee guidevare o'ye londe ye zwae,—t'avance pace an livertie, an, wi'oute vlynch, ee garde o' generale reights an poplare vartue. Ye pace —yea, we mai zei, ye vaste pace whilke bee ee-stent owr ye londe zince th'ast ee-cam, proo'th, y'at wee alane needeth ye giftes o'generale rights, az be displayte bie ee factes o'thie goveremente. Ye state na dicke daie o'ye londe, na whilke be nar fash nar moile, albiet 'constitutional agitation,' ye wake o'hopes ee-blighte, stampe na yer zwae be rare an lightzom. Yer name var zetch avancet avare ye, e'en a dicke var hye, arent whilke ye brine o'zea an ye craggès o'noghanes cazed nae balke. Na oure gladès ana whilke we dellt wi' mattoke, an zing t'oure caulès wi plou, wee hert ee zough o'ye colure o' pace na name o' *Mulgrave*. Wi Irishmen owre generale hopes be ee-bond—az Irishmen, an az dwellerès na cosh an loyale o' Baronie Forthe, w'oul daie an ercha daie, our meines an oure gurles, praie var long an happie zins, shorne o'lournagh an ee-vilt wi benisons, an yerzel an oure gude Zovereine, till ee zin o'oure daies be var aye be ee-go t'glade.

Figure 38 Hore's Speech in Yola

MAY IT PLEASE YOUR EXCELLENCY—We, the subjects of his Most Gracious Majesty, William IV, and, as we truly believe, both faithful and loyal inhabitants of the Barony of Forth, beg leave at this favourable opportunity to approach your Excellency, and in the simple dress of our old dialect to pour forth from the strength (or fulness) of our hearts, our sense (or admiration) of the qualities which characterise your name, and for which we have no words but of 'Governor', 'Statesman', &c. In each and every condition it is with joy of heart that our eyes rest upon the representative of that Sovereign, William IV, under whose paternal rule our days are spent; for before your foot pressed the soil, your name was known to us as the *friend of liberty*, and *he who broke the fetters of the slave*. Unto ourselves—for we look on Ireland to be our common country—you have with impartial hand ministered the laws made for every subject, without regard to this party or that. We behold in you one whose days are devoted to the welfare of the land you govern, to promote peace and liberty—the uncompromising guardian of common right and public virtue. The peace—yes, we may say the profound peace—which overspreads the land since your arrival, proves that we alone stood in need of the enjoyment of common privileges, as is demonstrated by the results of your government. The condition, this day, of the country, in which is neither tumult nor disorder, but that constitutional agitation, the consequence of disappointed hopes, confirms your rule to be rare and enlightened. Your fame for such came before you even into this retired spot, to which neither the waters of the sea below nor the mountains above caused any impediment. In our valleys, where we were digging with the spade, or as we whistled to our horses in the plough, we heard the distant sound of the wings of the dove of peace, in the word *Mulgrave*. With Irishmen our common hopes are inseparably bound up—as Irishmen, and as inhabitants, faithful and loyal, of the Barony Forth, we will daily and every day, our wives and our children, implore long and happy days, free from melancholy and full of blessings, for yourself and our good Sovereign, until the sun of our lives be gone down the dark valley (of death).

Figure 39 The translated speech

The translation, above, was supposed to mark the end of Yola as a written language, but events long after 1836, the soon to die date, changed the history of Yola.

Jump forward to 2018, surprisingly print Yola emerged again, so the dialect is not dead.

This mows down Yola's many obituary writers, in the 19th and 20 centuries.

Most people argue that Yola was last spoken in the Lady's Island, Carne, and Tachumshane areas, with the last Yola speaker being a Carnsore Point man, Martin Parlin, who lived to 90.

We don't really know if the dialect survived in the very remote Rosslare Fort, English was the main spoken language in the Fort, with its military, lifeboat crew, and Customs men, but some Yola was also spoken there, according to local historian, Shane Dunphy, and traditional dress survived among older women It may well have been that one family or two individuals spoke some Yola there up into the 20th century. We don't really know.

What we do know is the dialect last survived in remote coastal areas.

Last Yola spoken in Tachumshane

There is a rather charming tale reported about the death of Yola in the Tachumshane area, a remote, sparsely populated area a few miles inland from Rosslare. There are records that this is one of the areas where it was last spoken. Rev. Eastwood, a Tachumshane Church of Ireland clergyman, had local tradesmen repairing his house. The tradesmen spoke Yola among themselves, much to the fascination of the clergyman, who could not understand them.

By a coincidence, he had been reading Chaucer and recognised the similarity between Chaucer and Yola. He then assembled the workers and read them some of Chaucer's Canterbury Tales, which seemingly, they joyously understood.

Quite a charming tale!

What finally killed off Yola

The Taghmon Historical Society fingers an Educational Act as the hammer blow that killed off the dialect. This was Stanley's Irish Educational Bill 1830, this ushered in a new very successful era of literacy, but it excluded Yola and for that matter Irish, from the curriculum. Neither were there Yola or Irish language teachers involved in the new, very welcome, educational scenario.

It quickly replaced very low levels of literacy, in an era where quite a chunk of the population was illiterate and barefoot, and modern-day health systems did not exist.

Yoles were then excluded, with the Irish claiming they could not understand them, Irish speakers faced the same fate.

Figure 40 Picture from the History of the Franciscans in Wexford. The above is a woodcut of Wexford dated circa 1820 when Yola had started to go into decline.

A Yola Revival?

It is possible, from the words in this book, together with Poole's Glossary, for a reader to construct sentences and paragraphs, and speak and write some Yola, particularly with the fast expanding world of language apps, which changes for the better every month. Take a look at Duolingo.

Poole's Glossary is available free online.

There is nothing to prevent a small group, or one family, from attempting to speak Yola, pronunciation is going to be a problem, since the slow oral drawled delivery is a crucial aspect of the dialect, with the emphasis on the second syllable, or the end of a word.

This could be a fun exercise, and not a serious attempt at revival, just a novelty for people to swap a few Yola phrases. It could be attempted, like the tactic used by Irish language revivalists, by holding pop up sessions in pubs.

Interest in speaking Yola might not be confined to the south-east of Ireland, modern communication routes like YouTube could rapidly bring it to a wide audience, in the USA there is a modern fashion in learning the nearly dead dialects of the American Indian tribes. Most of the modern learners do not claim American Indian blood.

To go these local pop up, or YouTube routes, someone should devise modern interrogatory phrases, for its interrogatory phrases that elicit replies. What exists of Yola is agrarian, stuck in rural 19th century Forth and Bargy speak.

Modern phrases must be included in Yola.

- How are you?
- How is your Father?
- What is the Wi-Fi password?
- Will you buy an electric car?
- Did you buy a new mobile?
- Fine day
- Bad day
- Great match

Initial answers are likely to be in Yola, yes, or no.

As for *Wi-Fi*, or *electric car*, those words are probably best left in modern English with the speaker encouraged to emphasise the second syllable, or the end of the word. Electric car might end up as *electrik caar.*

As for language teaching, Benny Lewis is Irish and a polyglot, and he is making waves with his new language learning method, now being successfully applied. His idea is that to learn to ride a bike, you have to first try; if you fall off, you try and try again. There are no advance written lessons before you try to ride the bike, according to Lewis. He got all this together from his own experience in Spain, he initially worked and socialised with English speakers while teaching English, in that phase of his life in Spain, he learned zero Spanish.

When his English-speaking friends abruptly departed he was suddenly marooned, lost among Spanish speakers, he had no choice, but learn to ride- the- bike. He fell off the bike many times, but eventually, he learned to ride it and rapidly learned Spanish.

Lewis has turned language learning on its head, he says it is probable that the average person can become fluent in a language in three months. The learner has to start talking the language on Day 1, he says. There is no point in a delay while the student argues that they need words and grammar first, that they are not ready.

They will never be ready, Lewis argues.

Throwing conventional language teaching methods out the window, Lewis argues that the learner must speak the new language on Day 1, even if they sound like Tarzan, and they should be prepared to make 200 mistakes per day and be prepared to "sound like an idiot". Language learning must be fun, games, and films, should be included, he says.

Online you can see his free 10 step approach to language learning. He makes the point that natives of a country are patient when a learner approaches them on the street asking, *"me-go-supermarket*?". The learner is making himself understood, though he is not speaking the correct King's English.

Lewis is fluent in seven languages and speaks several more, he sees online and Skype as valuable language teaching tools.

Lewis argues that anyone can learn a language in three months.

Lewis's, or another fast learn method might just be the way to rejuvenate Yola.

Lewis has his critics, who dispute his fast track claims, but he also has very strong advocates, including Irish language teachers, who welcome him for his modern method. Irish language teachers are in a difficult position, trying to generate enthusiasm for a language in fast decline.

There are others apart from Lewis with fast-track language learning methods, including Lindsay Williams and more. Diverse fast-track learning teachers will likely emerge.

We had better not hold our breath for a Yola revival, but there may be some scope for the spreading of a few phrases, and from a Q and A session in Yola, let us see, what, - if anything develops?

Much is made of the correct pronunciation of Yola, the slow drawl, and emphasis on the second part, or end of a word. Perhaps if people attempt to speak a few Yola phrases, undue emphasis on pronunciation should be relaxed?

After all, Poles, Americans, and others, now speak Irish, with their very different accents, and pronunciation, not a problem for Irish speakers. The view being, among the Irish, that at least the Poles and Americans took the trouble to learn Irish. So, if a group attempts to speak a few phrases of Yola, correction of pronunciation among the group would probably be a very bad idea, instead, the group might ignore pronunciation, as the Irish generously do, with Polish and Americans speaking their language?

Lewis's Tarzan approach is probably the way to go, though that may annoy purists, who insist on the slow drawl.

The pronunciation purists hardly have much of a platform today with the dialect barely alive.

However, some spoken Yola is better than the situation today where little or practically no Yola is spoken.

Figure 41 image from WikiTongues

Above is, Ryan, from Ballymena, speaking in Yola on WikiTongues, one of the very few, if not the only digital view, cum spoken image of modern-day Yola. Ballymena, in Northern Ireland, is about 180 miles from Forth. WikiTongues is a global movement, aimed at boosting threatened dialects.

The European Charter for Regional or Minority Languages

This is an EU body, its member states sign up to, Ireland, for reasons that are unclear, has not signed up to this charter. So, this body does not cover Yola. Were Ireland to sign up, it is not clear if would benefit Yola.

The United Kingdom, a signatory, includes Cornish and Irish, as its minority languages, Spain another signature includes six languages among them Catalan and Basque.

Though English is the main language spoken in Ireland, a small number, around 30,000 speak Irish, a number that is fast dwindling. Online eats away at the Irish language. However, it is Government policy that Irish is the official language of Ireland. That may explain why Ireland has not signed.

It is confusing for non-Europeans to read that Britain lists Irish as a minority language, and that Ireland has not signed this Treaty.

Bargy today

While Yola seemingly died in Bargy in 1770, as the language of the parish, small phrases of Yola did survive. A woman who is very much alive today recounts her mother teaching her Yola phrases in the the 21st century. That woman immediately understood the first line of the song "The Maiden of Rosslare".

Liam O'Neill

On April 28[th,] 2018, the Irish Times gave Yola followers a severe shock, suggesting that the dialect did not die around 1870 as has been regularly reported. Yola followers are small in numbers, clinging to a belief it may still live, taking the line that it did it die out with the collapse of the Rosslare Fort in the late 1920s. The report in the Irish Times suggests there was at least one Yola speaker in the 1970s, an elderly man, living in Forth, who tried and seemingly did, pass on words, phrases, and songs to his grandson, Mr. O'Neill.

In 2018 he won a Hennessy Literary Award for this poem written in Yola, so it seems that Yola is not dead as we had been told.

Yola
Liam O'Neill

Ich loove ee mýdhe wee ee ribbonè blúe,
At coome to ee faaythè èar chee arichè too.

My father's father was a Yola Man,
born on the border of the baronies of Forth and Bargy,
in that great land of County Wexford,
or *Weisforthe* as it was called, in the Yola tongue.

In the summers of the 70s, my father took us to Forth
to visit his pater, who, by then, was an elderly man.
And our father's father spoke to us in strange vowels
and drawls and unusual placement of stress and emphasis.

'Quare hot day', he'd say, and the *'Zin be shinin' a heighe'*,
and then warning us of *'Them been in the treen'*,
Meaning 'take care of the nest of bees in the trees'.
It was words of Yola – the former mother tongue; a Middle English
    variant.

Brought, it is said, by Wessexmen; once 'settled' Normans
from the Shires of Somerset and Devon,
to the sunny southeast of Ireland,
then churned and stirred in a pot with Gaelic, Flemish and Manx.

He'd puff his pipe, then pause and open his mouth to recite,
parts he remembered of old Yola poem and song;
Ich loove ee mýdhe wee ee ribbonè blúe,
I love the maid with the ribbons blue,
At coome to ee faaythè èarchee arichè too,
That comes to the fair every morning too.

The old Yola man told stories of the Bargy people
who put *stuckeen* and *bhlock shoone* over their *toan*
and then on with their *cooat* and *garbe*
when marching off to *chourch* for *Zindei* mass.
And then, after taking leave of their *holies*, these Bargy people
ate *breed* and *caakes* topped off with *maate, baanes* and *bakoon.*

I always believed these words of Yola died with my father's father;
when his mouth closed for the last time
his lips sealed a tomb on a language
on a culture that was mortally wounded many generations before.

Now, older and capable of digging a little deeper, I see,
That some of the rural people of *Weisforthe*
still go, *wee sprong* to the *yole* meadow in the glade, and
sometimes *ate maate* and *baanes* and say *'How are ye?'*
and though the life and lexicon of a mother tongue is gone,
somehow, some words and their vowels, still struggle on.

Formerly an urban planner, Liam O'Neill is now a social care worker
and writer living in Galway city. He has had his work published in A
New Ulster and the Kilkenny Poetry Broadsheet. He has recently
published a non-fiction ebook on Amazon entitled *All the Days of
Winter*, a true story about one person's search for their mother.

Figure 42 From the Irish Times, April 2018

95

A Glossary of Yola Terms

Yola words and phrases

There are plenty of Yola words and phrases about, here are a few,

- *Ihause a der*, open the door, *theene a der,* close the door.
- *She's a goude lickeen michel.* She's a good looking woman.
- *Hea's a goude lickeen bye.* He is a good-looking boy
- *Ich am,* I am, *Ich as,* I was.
- Kircher bonnet
- *Nieght* night
- *A gaay wytheen*, a good-looking girl,
- *I ne wot* I know not.
- *'Ich knouth 'em*   I know him
- *Gaching* playing *Stop your gaching.* Stop your playing
- *A gorseyjack* a dandy young man, a man about town
- *Bockety* unsteady, a bockety chair
- *A schouch* A derogatory description of a young woman inferring she takes multiple lovers. *Schouchie Malcheen* Mary takes many lovers
- *Ty*, a drink, *Ty o' letch*, a drink of beer.
- *Runt*, rent or torn. *Mee coat is ee runt*, my coat is torn.
- *Teach* means To Hand or Give, *Teach mee.*
- *Be de hookey* A term of wonderment, still used today (This is probably Hollywood slang rather than Yola).
- *Dinna thar a dug* Don't vex the dog
- *Ishe*, a verb, to ask, *Dinna ishe wee   arison,* Dont ask me the reason
- *Kimmelt* cold or numbed *Mee hoanes is ee kimmelt* My hands are numbed with cold
- *Hamaron*, a horse collar, *Doost thou know fidi is a hameron,* Do you know where is the horse collar?
- *Ete,* a point of the compass, What ete does the wind blow from?
- *Bibber or Begger*, to shake or tremble, he was bibbering
- *Ayghteen,* the numeral 18.
- *Jock* a leather bucket used for serving ale

- *Holly* Holy *Hollydie* Holiday
- Gazb Gasp There is no gazb in him. He is dead.
- *Come adh o mee gazb.* Come out of my breath, or, get out of my way
- *Hougany* stupid A houghany *set* A stupid set
- *Zo wough kist an wough partet* So we kissed and parted
- *Awye wought it* Away with it
- *Venie* Dirty *Venie Bogher* A Dirty Road *Venie Shardh* A Dirty Gap
- *Veezer wiser Fhaade th' veezer*? What the wiser?
- *Ee-pealt a mydhe*   pelt, or beat the girl
- *Hele en grave apa thee*   Health and wealth to you
- *Unke*t strange unusual (and at least 10 other meanings)
- *Waaite* To attend *And wayten hire et festes* and at daunces
- *Waitier* waiter
- *Vidie?* Where? Only used in interrogation
- *Hatcheat* hatchet
- *Brover* brother *Sank Mogue is our brover*   St. Aidan is our brother
- *Zister* sister   Sank *Malcheen is our zister* St.Mary is our sister
- *Caul* horse
- *Co quo* quote used in quoting someone who is considered an authority *Co though* Quote thou *Co he* says he
- *Draugh* or *Drowe* to throw *Ich drove ham* I threw him
- *A bolsker*, a nasty or unpleasant person
- *Ammache* a dwarf
- Faade teit thee-zo lournagh What ails you, your so sad ?
- *Sleeveen* a rogue or nasty person, pronounced and spelled like the Irish word of the same meaning.
- *Laaace* Lace A daggere hagynge on a laace had he
- *Leiough* Idle   Leiough ut ee die Idle out the day
- *Kearnt* Ripening *Beanes is ee kearnt*   Beans are ripening

Yola Counting

English	Yola
One	Oan

97

Two	Twye
Three	Dhree
Four	Voure
Five	Weeve
Six	Zeese
Seven	Zeven
Eight	Ayght
Nine	Neen
Ten	Dhen
Twenty	Dwanty

Prepositions

English	Yola
Above	Aboo
Among	Amang
Around	Arent
About	Abit
At/bye	Adh/bee
Below/beneath	Aloghe
Between	Beewsk
For	Vor
From	Vrom
In	Ving
Out	Ut
With	Wee
Upon	Apan
Over	Ower
Through	Trugh

Pronouns and Determiners

English	Yola
Any	Aany
All	Aul
Each/every	Earchee

Few	Vew
None/nothing	Nodding
Some	Zim
This/that	Dhickei/dhicka

Grammar

First Person		
	Sing	Plural
Nom	Ich	Wee/wouk
Acc	Me	Ouse
Gen	Mee	Oure

Second Person		
	Sing	Plural
Nom	Thou	Ye
Acc	Theeu	Ye
Gen	Thee	Yer

Third Person		
	Sing	Plural
Nom	Hea, Shoo	Thye, hi
Acc	Him, her, it	Aam
Gen	Hi	Aar

Days of the Week

English	Yola
Monday	Mondie
Tuesday	Tuesedi
Wednesday	Wennesedi
Thursday	Thorsdei

Friday	Vreedie
Saturday	Zathardei
Sunday	Zindei

Yola Words That Activate With English

English	Yola
What	Fade
Who	Fho
Where	Fidi
When	Fan
Which	Wich
Why	Farthoo
How	Towe

Other Words

English	Yola
Sun	Zin
Land	Loan
Wexford	Westforthe
Day	Dei/die
Friend	Vriene
Yourself	Theezil
The	a/ee
Thing	Dhing
Go	Ee/go
Fear	Vear
Old	Yola/yole

Yola First Names

English	Yola
Patrick	Parick
Anne or Nanny	Naneen
Mogue or Aidan	Moake

Margaret	Margraate
Mary	Malcheen
Joseph	Josef
Michael	Kealeen or Kealy
James	Jaames
Joan or Judy	Jauaaan
Jane	Jennate
Sarah	Zailee
Peter	Beedheer
Miles	Milchare
Robert or Robin	Rubbeen
Simon	Zimoon
Elen	Neleen
Tadhg	Theig
Little John or Little Sean	Shaneen
William	Wyllhaume

Yola conversational phrases

- *Fare* Frighten *Dinna fare a caules* Dont frighten the horses
- *Tartha Yarthe How yarth to-die, mee joee*? How art thou today my joy?
- *Saaughe* Comfortable *Myne Saaughe* Very comfortable
- *Note* A contradiction for *I new wot*, I know not *Note vidy*, I do not know where
- *Deen* Dress *Deen theezil* Dress yourself
- *Vleash or Viesh Flesh Bileta viesh* Boiled meat or boiled mate
- *Winnoween* Blowing in the *wind The condel is to winnoween* The wind is blowing the candle. Winnowing ia also a grain crop harvesting term.
- *Lidge* Lie or lay *Woughlidg'd we lay Lidge w'ous*. Lie or lodge with us
- *Yola Zong* A Yola song *Yola Teung* a Yola town
- *Lyght* Light *Lyght water*, light water
- *Saaaughe* at ease, comfortable
- *Myne saaugghe* very comfortable
- *Quiel laaune* a lively smart fellow

- Kesse Kiss   And hire in armes took and gan hire kesse
- *Hele* Health *Your Hele* Your Health a toast
- *Ee-go* Gone *He's eg go* He is gone
- *Blin* Mistaken Ich *as* or *chas greatky bin* I was greatly mistaken
- *Agone* In the past. *What his ire is thus agoon*
- Haail Hale, be Healthy Haail Maree Hail Mary
- *Ishe* To ask. *Dinna ishe mee a raison.* Don't ask me a reason
- *Scaul* scald *Scaule hoate* scalding hot
- *Kun* a brazen faced or ugly woman
- *Coarhed* searched *Coarhed an recoardhed* Searched and recorded
- Coome come Coome thee wyse Come thy ways
- *I herde a swogh*   I heard a sigh
- Weithe lookest or seemest *Ty weithest*   Thou lookest
- *Mell* Meddle *Dinna mell wi' it'* Don't meddle with it
- *Aager* acre of land *Dhen aager* ten acres
- Been bees They murmureden as doth a swarm of been
- *Busk* seems to have two meanings, the first a type of cake or caake, the *second, a small goat stringed musical Instrument, now called a bowran. Busk* may have evolved into busker, the modern day description of a street musician
- *Zea* sea
- *Palsk* a type of cake

More Yola words and phrases

- *Brogue* old fashioned shoe, also means accent, brogue is also the Irish word for a shoe. *Keowe* is another Yola word for a shoe
- LLoan land Engelloan England Erelhoan Ireland
- Maake to make Maake why make way
- *Leech* doctor
- *Attercop* spider when applied to a person, a derogatory term
- *Baakooze* bake house
- *Aalhouse* alehouse, or pub

- *Unket* This Yola word has 12 meanings in English, strange, unfamiliar, uncouth, odd, shy, ill-bahaved, unknown, akward, ugly, inconvenient, untidy. and shy.
- *Telgence* intelligence or news
- *Usquebaugh* whiskey, quite like the Irish word for whiskey
- *Vinger* finger
- *Reicht* right *reicht vinger* right finger r*eicht hoane* right hand *reicht aarm*
- *Spud* knife also means potato *Kunnife* is another Yola word for a knife
- *Sarree* A term of contempt
- *Woul* wish *Ich woul ich had* I wish I had
- *Whil* capsize *Whileen to thee* A mild polite curse, may you fall on your head
- *Gouger* a person of criminal intent best avoided, centuries ago it meant a Customs man with no criminal inference.
- Earnough droll *A gooude earnough* A droll man
- *Gabble* chatter he gabbled on
- *Kimlear* an akward person
- *Leet* a meeting point of roads *A four way leet* crossroads
- *Houze* or *Heouse* both mean house
- *Hulmogue* cabinet
- Greve grove He looketh forth by, by tre, by greve
- Ellena ghou elder tree treo hongede him after
- *Fare* frighten *Dinna fare a cauls* Don't frighten the horses
- *Ac when smoke ans smorthre smyt in hus eyen* smoke smothered his eyes
- *Smaddereen* a small quantity, of *aal* or *usquebaugh* a small measure of ale or whiskey
- *Vat* fat
- Yole or Yola teun Yola town Yola zong Yola song

- *Gagee* or *Gauger* An excise man. *Gauger* has now evolved into meaning gangster, or a person to be avoided . A person of criminal intent.
- *Hist* a fist *Twy histfulles*   two fistfuls
- *Ropeare* a brawler. A *ropeare* and a *gauger*, a person to be avoided for two reasons
- *Blin* mistaken *chas greatly blin* I was greatly mistaken
- Coarhed searched   *coarhed an recoardhed* searched and researched
- Burdes or Fowls birds
- *Chemis* manor house
- *Bred* bread
- *Co, Quo* said, quote. *Co thou* quote thou   *Co he* says he
- *'Cha* I have
- *'Cham* I am
- *'Chas* I was
- *'Chull*   I will
- *Dest na* do not
- *Dhica* this, that *dhicka poake* that pocket
- Gee Goeth   to go
- *Scuudeen*   a shrug
- *'Far yersthei*   ere yesterday
- *Sheakeare* a seriously under grown young man, a runt.
- Zough a deep sigh I herde a swogh
- *Vat* vinger fat finger
- *Gom* a fool
- *Gurl* girl
- *Ich drove ham* I threw him   *drowe* or *draugh* means to throw
- *His eyen greye as glass*   his eyes as grey as glass
- *Baekoon* bacon
- 'Hea's ee-go'   He is gone
- *Zweal*   ruckus or commotion
- *Pa ooree* upon each other *Pa cawl*   upon the horse Pa means upon

- *I ne wot* I know not
- *Note vidy* I do not know where
- *Note will wee dra aaght to-die?* I don't know will we draw any today?
- Paugh-meale kissing time
- *Vrosth* frost
- *Waudher* water
- *Vale a danceen* set at dancing
- *Vour wing leet* four cross roads
- *Chas mhyne weery* I was very weary *whyne* means very
- *Curthere* season
- *Arraugh curthere* the Spring.
- *Zummer curthere* the Summer.
- *Harresr curthere* the Autumn
- *Wonter curthere* the Winter
- *Chugh* clown
- *Cub* a small young male or boy or trainee boy
- Vurst first
- *Wich* which
- Wich ad wough beththter kwingokee or baahchoose vurst? Had we better churn or bake first?
- *Leather* or *Luther* to beat *Leathered gurl. Pelted gurl* A girl hit by thrown fruit.
- *Heste* behest
- *Withoute bode his heste* she obeyed
- *Mot w'all aar boust hi soon was eeteight* But with all their bravado they were soon taught.
- *Many a bra draught by Tommeen was ee-maate* Many a brave stroke by Tommy was made
- *Na,now or neveare* Nay, now or never!
- *Zo bless all oore frends, an God zpeed ee plowe.* So bless all our friends, and God speed the plough.
- *Zoo wough aul a-danceen* So we all fell a dancing

- *Earch bye gae a poage*   Each boy gave a kiss
- *Y'oure w' thee crookeen, an yi mee thy hoane*   Give over your crossness, and give me your hand
- *Ye be welcome, heartilee welcome, mee joes* You are welcome heartily welcome, my joys.
- *Ye be welcome hearthilee, ivery oan.* You are heartily welcome, every one
- *Lidge w'ouse an a milagh, tis gay an louthee* Lie with us on the clover, 'tis fair and sheltered.
- *Ha deight ouse var gabble, tell ee zin go t'glade* You have put us in talk, 'till the sun goes to set.
- *'Tis gay an louthee*   Tis fair and sheltered
- *Caroles* Christmas carols
- *Comman* a hurley stick, a curved hockey like stick used in the Irish game, hurling, The goal keeper in that game is called the *cowlee man* in Yola.
- *Fade teil thee zo lournagh* ?   What ails you so melancholy *?*
- *Don* to put on. He donned his hat
- *Grig* to tantalise, a phrase about a young woman exciting a young man
- *Rooze* to rouse
- Th' weithest You seem
- *Th' weithest all curcagh*   You seem all snappish
- *Th' weithest all curcagh, wafur, an cornee.* You seem all snappish, uneasy, and fretfull.
- *Th' valler w' speen here, th' less ee church-hey.*   The more we spend here, the less in the churchyard.
- *At by mizluck was ee-pit t'drive in.* Who by misluck was placed to drive in.
- *Huck nigher.* Come nearer
- *Fartoo zo haches ?* Why so ill tempered ?
- *Jaane got leigheen.*   Joan set them a laughing
- *Shoo pleast aam all.* She pleased them all.

- *Yie mee thee hoan*. Give me your hand.
- *A peepeare struck ap, wough dancsth aul in a ring.* A piper struck up and we danced in a ring.
- *Var whither than snow.*   Far whiter than snow.
- *Zoo wough kisth, an wough parthet.* So we kissed and we parted.
- *Dhicka cursed vox.* That cursed fox.
- *A plaauge apan Portheare.* A plague upon Porter. A serious nasty cursing phrase.
- *Ich aam goan make mee will.*   I am going to make my will.
- *He daffed his coat*. He took off his coat.
- *He doffed his hat*   He raised his hat, an old fashioned respectfull salute
- *'Cham afear'd ich mosth crossa Shannon an lea a parish o Kilmannan'*.I am afraid I must cross the Shannon, and leave the parish of Kilmannan.
- *Amain* going on *amain* getting on well
- *Drazed* threadbare or exhausted
- *Keep* to peep
- *Vather* Father, with the pronunciation distinctly on a long a, or double a *Vaather*
- *Moodher* Mother
- Vreedie Friday Gooude Vreedie Good Friday
- *A Slouk* An idle person
- *Shilleen* shilling
- Keow a cow
- *Potion* dowry
- *A potion ich gae her was keow an dwanty shilleen* The dowry I gave her was a   cow and twenty shilllings
- Bring-awn limpet
- *Glade* Sunset   goan to glade Sunsetting *gone to glade* after Sunset
- *Hoornta* Horned *Hornta beast* a horned beast
- *Hele* Health *Yer hele* your health, a toasting drinking term

- *Frump* To scold, jeer, also confusingly, it also seems to mean, a contrary old woman, the link may be that the contrary old woman would scold.
- Pussough plump or thick *A pussoughe mydhe* a plump girl a *Pussoughe cake* a large cake, a *caake*
- *Pilleen* a womans saddle
- *Breed* bread
- *Hempeen* a little bird
- Huske a flock
- *Buy* boy
- Weddeen wedding
- *Breekvast* breakfast
- *Stuckeen* stocking
- *Praiscin* apron,(there seems to be at least three other Yola words for apron)
- *Skewlune* an apron worn for farm work
- Y,cleped named
- *Amize* Amaze
- Sippeare Supper
- Meyen Women Blessed yarth among meyen
- *Vaapereen* Boasting *Vaaper* a brager
- Spone spoon
- *Shoone* shoes
- Shoone maakeare shoe maker
- *Priesth* priest
- Coo-pen cow byre
- *Nuggeen* a noggin, drink measure
- *Koornt* corned or preserved
- *Koornt mate* corned meat
- *Lloan* island
- *Praate* talk on and on, she *praated* on about Little John
- *A Kimleare* an akward person
- *Hey* a fenced area

- *Chourch hey* a churchyard
- *Jooudge* a judge
- *Houze* a house
- *Vole* house
- *Fowel* Birds *Fowler* A hunter of birds *Burdes* is another Yola word for birds
- *And small foweles maken melodye* And small birds make melody
- *Greash* Grace *Greash an'goouness* Grace and Goodness
- *Ich am* I am *Ich as* I was *Ich will* I will
- *Heigh* sky
- *Dhurth* Rain, or dirt or sleet *Ar's dhurth a heighe* There is dirt in the sky
- *Ee go* Gone *Hea's ee go* He is gone
- *Gendrize* Gentry
- *Dereling* Darling *I am thyn Absolon my deerelyng*
- *Aught* Anything *Geet hea aught ?* Did he get anything?
- *Truckle* an older designed cart *A truckle is ee-teap'd'* The cart is overturned.
- *Almosty ee go* mostly gone
- *Bawen* a safe enclosure for cattle
- Goouun gun
- *Grenge* grange or mill
- *Kink* to toss or trip up
- *Zhip* ship
- *A Wad* a bundle, of hay, or Pound notes
- *Dhosure* A wad or fistful of money
- *Vull* full
- Vull o' Graace full of Grace Haail Malcheen vull o' grace Hail Mary full of grace
- *A war cowdealeen wi ooree'* they were scolding with each other
- Noucht none
- *Zoot* soot

- Condale candle *The condale is to winnoween* The wind is blowing the candle
- *Patroon* patron
- *Borde* table
- Woul wish   *Ich woul ich had*   I wish I had
- Veeser   Wiser   Fhaade th' veeser what the wiser
- *Poumgaam* a cry of grief
- *Vire* fire
- *Whil* upset   *Whileen to thee*   That you may be upset, a mild polite curse.
- Smockeen smoking
- *Straung* strong
- *Mize* amaze
- *Outh* out
- *Outh o' harr* out of joint, or mad
- *Piz poraches* peace porridge
- *Pee* pie
- *Fho* who?
- *Fho told thee?* Who told thee?
- *Furloan* a rocky path into the sea. The furloan at Kilmore Quay
- *Fest* fist
- *And on the nose he smoot hym with his fest.* And on the nose he hit him with his fist
- *Vour* four
- *Vour wing leet* four cross roads
- *Teil* ail
- *Fad teil?* what ails?
- Hardish A thing
- *hardish o' anoor* One thing or another

Old Bannow words and phrases

Grantstown historian, Father C. Butler, published a remarkable list of words and phrases from the Carrick-on –Bannow area, in south-west Wexford, in a book titled, A Parish and its People, he divides these rare words from Yola, even though Carrick on Bannow is in Bargy, where Yola was spoken.

THE LONG STONE

(C. 2500 B.C.)

at Balloughton

Figure 43 a photo of Fr. Butler, standing to the right of the Long Stone in Bannow the photo is from a Parish and its People

Some of these unique old words and phrases seem to be in use today.

He argues, Bannow people use the word, *doubt*, where they mean, certain or sure. Shall we have rain? *I doubt we will.*

It is your *steven* now? Meaning it is your turn now?

Local people used the word *great* to mean, fine or splendid. She had a great hat on her yesterday.

The word *dull* was used to mean attachment. He was dull about reading this while back. Or she was dull about that bicycle of hers.

Instead of using the normal English phrase, become aware of, Bannow people used the word, *war*. When he was cycling down the hill he *warred* the brake was gone.

Some of the local words borrow directly from Irish, while Yola borrowed from words imported from England during the Norman invasion. Thus in Bannow people used the word, *be's*, as a direct translation of the Irish habitual "bim". He *be's* crying going to school.

Mrs S. C. Hall and her Bannow phrases

Father Butler noticed phrases in the works of Mrs S.C. Hall (1800-1881) the celebrated writer, who spent her formative years in Bannow until moving to London when she was 14.

Fr. Butler goes on

Card players used local words like *hove*. Who *hoved* the diamonds, or I will *hove* a trump.

When it was mentioned there was no *heech* in the pump that meant no water to be got by pumping.

If a car *taped* at the cross, it meant it spun on two wheels or turned over.

The local word *waurs* was substituted for feeling, I'll put on my hat for *I waurs the cold*.

The omission of the word *to* after *going*. It's going rain

He *hedged* it on to John, he passed the blame onto John

Use of the word *brave* to mean fine or very. He is brave and well this morning

The word *scootch* to mean ride. He scootched down to Kilmore

The word *reckon* was used instead of count. I must reckon the sheep.

The word *took* is used instead of overtook, he took up on us going down the hill

Use of *way* instead of towards. He is gone the way of the village

As for Irish words used in Bargy, this is what Fr. Butler wrote,

Although at one time the baronies of Forth and Bargy had at a dialect of their own, known as Yola, a remnant of old Flemish, yet many words from old Irish survived the centuries as well, in spite of the fact that Irish was not spoken in the area since the coming of the Normans. It could well be that they came in from outside the baronies but it must be remembered that the natives of both baronies kept very much to themselves and had very little contact with the native Irish.

Many of the words given here are taken from the book, *Sketches of Bannow,* by Mrs S.C. Hall, and were in common use in Bannow up until about 170 years ago.

Fr. Butler goes on to mention these Irish words, including agra, accousla, and avourneen, which sound straight out of the Irish language dictionary, Dinneen, other words less so. Words that are common to Yola, Irish, and English include park, chick, gossoon, and colcannan, the Irish vegetable dish.

- *Bocher* beggerman
- *Bouclawn* ragword
- *Bresnaugh* a bundle of fire wood
- *Bunyuck* the last person to tie a sheaf in the harvest
- *Collouge* conspire. You collouged against him
- *Clooricaun*   a fairy
- *Coshur*   a youngster looking for an egg
- *Doodeen*   a clay pipe, in Irish, *duidin*
- *Doshure*   a fistful of money
- *Dawshy* seems to mean dashing or stylish. Your dawshy shoes, or dawshy Aunt.
- *Flahulagh*   generous
- *Gumshogue* nonsense.   What a load of gumshogue
- *Grawls* means children. The grawls were playing
- Grasnogue the meaning of this word is unclear. "more like a grasnogue than a Christian " is how Fr. Butler uses it.

- *Hourishing* a word addressed to pigs when they were being fed.
- *Luskawn* the joint in the binding of a sheaf
- *Ownshuck* a fool or simple person
- *Praiscin* apron, confusingly, there are several different Yola words for an apron
- *Spillogue* an untidy person
- *Streale* an untidy woman
- *Sugan* a straw rope
- *On the Shaughrawn* wandering from place to place
- *Skewlune* yet another word for apron, the skewlune was an apron used when picking potatoes
- *Spalpeen* a good-for-nothing person
- *Thackeen* a young woman
- *She hushowed her little charge to sleep* she lulled her child to sleep
- *Bawngarr* a short field
- *Banscog* meaning not known, quite refreshing to hear historians do not know!
- *Bawnasheeogue* the field of the fairies
- *Bawlleendoon* townland of the fort
- *Beltin Hill* the hill where beltin, or the burning of the stubble, was practised
- *Croompawns* seemingly two meanings, a tree trunk, or a sea inlet
- *Gortaphillia* the field of the watercress
- *Goneens* a sandy path
- *Hye* a generic term for a field, said to be Flemish, such as hy me lye, near Cullenstown
- *Meenach* a place of mineral wealth
- *Monnymore* a great thicket
- *Poulmona* the boghole
- *Parkeen* a small field
- *Parkmore* a big field
- *Parish field* a field in a wood, set aside by a landlord, from where his tenants can take away free fuel

- *Shankyle* an old wood
- *Scruit* a first crop meadow, never mowed, but grazed
- *Shambles* a slaughter house
- *Weeping hill* a road full of water springs

Medieval pronunciations of words in common usage

- *Tay tea*,
- *wake* weak
- *mate* meat
- *sowl* soul
- *hate* heat
- *bate* beat
- *floore* floor
- *doore* door

All the above were collected and published by Fr. Butler in 1985, a distinguished historian, he hardly made it all up, neither did Mrs. Hall. While there seems to be little interest today in Fr. Butler's collected words and phrases, to some extent this may be due to the publishing date, ahead of the birth of the Web, as we know it, and language chat forums, were he alive today, he probably would be getting some attention on the Web. Interestingly, he argues that Yola is Flemish, most other historians point to west of England origins.

References and sources

- Centenary Record, published Wexford 1958
- a Parish and its People, by Rev C Butler, O.S.A. permission to research copy and use photos, from the O.S.A order.
- A Glossary of the Old Dialect of the English Colony in the Baronies of Forth and Bargy, formerly collected by Jacob Poole, edited by T.P. Dolan and Diarmaid O Muirithe, of University College Dublin, in the Journal of the Ui Cinsealaigh Historical Society, Volume 13, 1979.
- Wexford, a Town and its Landscape, by Billy Colfer, Cork University Press, 2008.
- Glossologics
- Languagehat.com This is a well-respected website, it suggests some Yola was spoken in Forth in the 1970's, and that people in Forth in the 1960's alarmed at the decline of the dialect, made (unstated) efforts towards its survival. That 1960's initiative remains unclear.
- English Irish, and Irish English dictionaries
- Know thy place Blog, Irelands forgotten languages
- RTE Radio 1, Yola, lost for Words, by Shane Dunphy
- Geoffrey Chaucer Quotes; Goodreads, Brainyquote, Wikipedia
- Chaucer Gloss Art
- Filthy Chaucer, Guardian
- Dank Chaucer Slang
- Extended Chaucer research
- The Proper English Foundation Yola Blog
- JSTOR Blog, An Account of the Barony of Forth, in the County of Wexford
- Yola Omniglot forum
- Journal of the Wexford Historical Society, Rosslare Fort and its People, Gerard Kehoe, 1974/1975.
- Same Jnl. Photo, Dr. G. Hadden, 1968. The Dash Churn, drawing, same Jnl. Miss M. Conboy 1968.
- Same Jnl. 1984-1985 Tobacco Growing, by Dr. Mary Gwinnell

- Irish Dialects Past and Present, by T.F. O Rahily. 1932, Browne and Nolan
- The Datai Discussion Forums
- An Account of the Barony of Forth 17th century, Vol. 4, No 1, Kilkenny Archaeological Society, 1862.
- The Globalization of Irish traditional song performance, by Dr. Susan H. Motherway, 2013, Ashgate Pubs.
- The Anglo-Normans and their English dialect of south-east Wexford, the English language in Ireland, Mercier Press, 1977.
- The Dialects of Forth and Bargy, T.P. Dolan, and D. O Muirithe, Four Courts Press
- Yolawiki

Thank You

Many people contributed to this book, which started out as an account of a dead dialect, which is not true. Numerous conversations over many years kept up this authors interest in the dialect.

- My wife, Esther Murnane, has been patient over the years, she saw the Yola Poem in the Ticket in April 2018, which reshaped this book.
- My nephew, Jim Gleeson, encouraged this work and suggested a map of Forth and Bargy be included.
- Ray Whelan has been patient in inserting images into the text.
- Bill Gleeson, my nephew, has been patient in his computer assistance, and at one stage rescued the entire text of the book, lost by this author in cyber space.
- The National Gallery of Ireland has provided magnificent images depicting the life style of centuries past in Ireland.
- Whyte's the Dublin art auctioneers for producing such excellent catalogues.
- The Ros Tapestry for permission to publish three of its works
- The Ticket, part of the Irish Times, for its Yola poem, part of the Hennessy Awards

25082295R00071

Printed in Great Britain
by Amazon